THE PARACLETE

A SERIES OF DISCOURSES ON THE PERSON
AND WORK OF THE HOLY SPIRIT

BY

WILLIAM CLARK

M.A., LL.D., D.C.L., F.R.S.C.

Professor of Philosophy in Trinity University,
Toronto.

THE SLOCUM LECTURES 1899, DELIVERED AT
THE UNIVERSITY OF MICHIGAN

TORONTO
GEORGE N. MORANG & COMPANY LIMITED
1900

Printing Statement:

Due to the very old age and scarcity of this book,
many of the pages may be hard to read due to the
blurring of the original text, possible missing pages,
missing text, dark backgrounds and other issues
beyond our control.

Because this is such an important and rare work, we
believe it is best to reproduce this book regardless of
its original condition.

Thank you for your understanding.

PREFACE.

Whatever may be the defects of this volume, it has not been undertaken without a deep sense of the greatness of its subject, nor yet without earnest and protracted study. The writer may claim to have made himself acquainted with all the principal treatises on the Holy Spirit, both ancient and modern ; and he puts forth his own contribution to the subject in the hope that there may be found in it some evidence of independent thought and work.

Twelve years ago the writer was appointed by Bishop Harris, a most distinguished member of a great Episcopate, to deliver the second series of Baldwin Lectures, the first having been given by the beloved Dr. Cleveland Coxe, Bishop of Western New York. It is with a deep sense of the high honor again conferred upon him that he has undertaken this work entrusted to him by the revered and accomplished successor of Bishop Harris, the Right Reverend Dr. Davies.

WILLIAM CLARK.

Trinity College, Toronto,
Advent, 1899.

CONTENTS.

THE
CHARLOTTE WOOD SLOCUM
LECTURES.

The Charlotte Wood Slocum lectureship on "Christian Evidences" was endowed in 1890 by the lamented lady whose name it bears, the wife of Elliott T. Slocum, Esq., of Detroit, in grateful memory of the life and labours of the Right. Rev. Samuel Smith Harris, D.D., LL.D., the second Bishop of Michigan. Mrs. Slocum departed this life in Dresden, 6th June, 1891. Bishop Harris —to quote his own words—"moved by the importance of bringing all practical Christian influences to bear upon the great body of students annually assembled at the University of Michigan, undertook to promote and set in operation a plan of Christian work at said University, and collected contributions for that purpose, of which plan the following outline is here given, that is to say :

To erect a building or hall near the University, in which there should be cheerful parlours, a well-equipped reading-room, and a lecture-room, where the lectures hereinafter mentioned might be given ;

To endow a Lectureship similar to the Bampton Lectureship in England, for the establishment and defence of Christian truth, the lectures on such foundation to be delivered at Ann Arbor by a learned clergyman or other communicant of the Protestant Episcopal Church;

To endow two other Lectureships: one on Biblical Literature and Learning, and the other on Christian Evidences, the object of such Lectureships to be to provide for all the students who may be willing to avail themselves of a complete course of instruction in sacred learning and in the philosophy of right thinking and right living, without which no education can justly be called complete.

The first of the Lectureships projected by Bishop Harris, that for the establishment and defence of Christian truth, was endowed in 1886 by the Hon. Henry P. Baldwin and wife. The second to be founded is that on Christian Evidences, and it is in fulfilment of the earnest wish of the founder that the first course is given by the Rev. John Fulton, D.D., LL.D. The lecturer is appointed upon the nomination of the Bishop of Michigan.

As Mrs. Slocum executed no deed of trust when she placed in my hands ten thousand dollars for the object above named, I have thought it advisable to appoint as Trustees of this fund those gentlemen who are charged with the trust of the foundation for the Baldwin Lectureship, viz.: Messrs. Henry P. Baldwin, Henry A. Hayden, Sidney D. Miller, Henry P. Baldwin, 2nd, Hervy C. Parke, with the addition of Mr. Elliott T. Slocum.

THOMAS F. DAVIES,

Bishop of Michigan.

Detroit, November, 1891.

LECTURE I.

THE HOLY GHOST VERY GOD

Man's need of God. God may be known. God one and three. I. The Doctrine of the Trinity gradually revealed. II. Divinity and Personality of the Holy Spirit. 1. Divinity.—(1) Name of God given; (2) Divine attributes and actions ascribed; (3) Worker of Miracles. 2. Personality.—(1) Testimony of Gospels, specially words of Christ. (2) Acts of Apostles; (3) Epistles. III. History of the Doctrine; Council of Constantinople. IV. Procession of Holy Spirit. Double Procession. Importance of the doctrine.

A LL history testifies to the existence, in the human race, of an inextinguishable long- ing for a knowledge of God. Oftentimes the enquiry may seem to be abandoned in despair. Men have been ready to confess that the mystery of the Godhead was unsearchable, and to cry out : "Canst thou by searching find out God ? Canst thou find out the Almighty unto perfection ? "* And the answer has come back : " We cannot find Him out unto perfection. This mystery is 'higher than heaven' and 'deeper than hell :' how then can we know it ?" In the grand

*Job xi, 7.

language of Hooker :* "Dangerous it were for
the feeble brain of man to wade far into the
doings of the Most High; whom although to
know be life, and joy to make mention of His
name; yet our soundest knowledge is to know
that we know Him not as indeed He is, neither
can know Him. . . . . . . He is above, and we
upon earth; therefore it behoveth our words to
be wary and few."

Such thoughts should ever be with us when
we take in hand to explore the mysteries of the
Godhead. Yet they should never be suffered to
press so heavily upon us as to paralyse our
spiritual energies and drive us to hopelessness.
Man is himself divine, although finite, and therefore he may know something of the Divine.
Although no man hath seen God at any time,
yet the only begotten Son hath declared Him;
and that Son has said : " He that hath seen Me
hath seen the Father."† To refuse the revelation which God has given, therefore, is no proof
of humility, but of arrogance. The agnostic is
merely interposing his own wilfulness in order
to shut out the light which descends from
heaven. God has truly revealed Himself; and,
although our knowledge of Him can never

*" Eccles. Pol.," i. 2, 2.
†St. John, xiv. 9.

be complete, yet, as far as it goes, it may be true and adequate.

Now, the revelation of God which we have received is a revelation at once of Unity and Trinity. "Our God," says the same great writer, "is One, or rather very Oneness, and mere unity, having nothing but itself in itself, and not consisting (as all things do besides God) of many things. In which essential Unity of God, a Trinity personal nevertheless subsisteth, after a manner far exceeding the possibility of man's conceit."

Here, then, is our starting point : the unity of God, the central truth of Holy Scripture and of the Christian Church, and the principle of all true religious worship. That there is one Being above all others, in whom all things subsist, uncreated, self-existent, eternal, infinite, is not only the faith which is consciously held by all who worship the living and true God, but it is a belief which has always been shared, although dimly and indistinctly, even by polytheists and idolaters. It has been remarked that men who professed to believe in "gods many and lords many," have yet in their hours of danger invoked the one God and Lord of all; and one of the greatest minds of the Church of Christ has told us that the heathen had never fallen so utterly under the belief of false gods as to have lost the idea of the one God from whom all things proceed *

If, however, we accept the testimony of the Christian Scriptures, we shall conclude that God is not only Unity, but Trinity in Unity. They tell us of a Father who reveals Himself through the Son and by the Holy Spirit. The writers of the New Testament employ language concerning the Son and the Holy Spirit which is intelligible only on the supposition that each of these Persons is, equally with the Father, Very and Eternal God. The Holy Scriptures set before us the history of those events in the development of the human race, and in the dealings of Almighty God with His creatures, in which He has revealed and declared His own Name and Nature and Attributes. The revelation of the Holy Ghost was, so to speak, the last word in this series of disclosures. It completed the revelation of the doctrine of the Holy Trinity.

For many years there has been a wide-spread feeling in the Church that the doctrine of the Holy Ghost does not hold its due place either in

---

*"Gentes non usque adeo ad falsos deos esse delapsas, ut opinionem amitterent unius veri Dei, ex quo est omnis qualiscunque natura." S. August. *C. Faust.* l. 20, n. 19, Cf. Hooker, l. c.

the teaching of the Church or in the life of its members. During the last few years a good deal has been done to wipe away this reproach. The deepening of the study of theology has brought the conviction that the ignoring of the work of the Spirit is the mutilating of the doctrine of Christ ; and treatises not a few have been put forth giving evidence of deep meditation and enlightened thought on this great subject. Nevertheless, there is still much to be done. There are still many religious and devout minds who are unable to rise above the conception of the Divine Spirit as an influence or energy ; and this undeniable fact is an evidence of the need of more careful instruction on the subject. On the importance of the doctrine it is not necessary to insist. Either the Holy Ghost is very God, of one substance with the Father and the Son, or the Church Universal has been in error for many centuries. It is sufficient merely to state such an alternative in order to point out the greatness of the question now before us.

The Holy Ghost is very God—we have deemed it best to take this fundamental doctrine as our starting point ; and, before proceeding to deal directly with the doctrine itself, it may be helpful first to say something on the doctrine of the Holy Trinity, which is inseparably connected with it. Indeed it is obvious that the demonstration of the doctrine of the Trinity necessarily involves the proof of the Godhead of the Holy Ghost; and, on the other hand, we cannot completely satisfy ourselves on the doctrine of the third Person in the Holy Trinity without having regard to the relations of the Three Persons. As, however, our principal concern here is with the truth of the Divine Spirit, the general doctrine will receive somewhat brief consideration.

i. Now, in considering a doctrine so mysterious and so awful as that of the Holy Trinity in the Unity of the Godhead, we must bear in mind that we are dealing not with mathematical truth which is the subject of demonstration, nor with observed fact which can be definitely proved by testimony, but with spiritual truth which needs a certain moral and spiritual preparation for its reception, and with a particular truth which, after being obscurely intimated, was gradually made known as men were prepared for its reception.

As regards the doctrine of the Holy Trinity, it is beyond question that it was not clearly revealed to mankind for a long period of time, whilst it is hardly possible to deny that there were certain anticipations of the doctrine in the beliefs of earlier ages. It is not difficult in some degree

to understand what we may call the reticence
of Divine Revelation on this subject. It is not
merely that all the nations of antiquity were
afflicted with polytheism, and that the chosen
people themselves were frequently falling into
the superstitions and idolatries of the nations
round about them. For these reasons alone it
might have been judged expedient to keep back,
for a season, a doctrine which might have fostered such errors among a people whose spiritual
education was necessarily imperfect. But there
were other reasons. If the truth concerning the
Divine Nature had been made known in earlier
times, it must have been revealed nakedly, and
apart from those facts which alone could give
it significance and power, and apart from that
prolonged religious discipline and education by
which it was actually introduced to the knowledge of men. Almighty God makes truth known
to his creatures as they are able to receive it, to
turn it to practical account, to profit by it, and
so it was in the revelation of the Holy Trinity.

On these principles we can understand what
is the kind of evidence which may reasonably
be expected in support of this mysterious doctrine. It would obviously be quite unreasonable
to expect, in the earlier periods of Divine Revelation, such clear intimations of the doctrine as

we find in the fully developed teaching of the apostles of Christ. Those who call in question the truth of the doctrine because it was unknown to patriarchs and Hebrews, can hardly have apprehended the principle of Divine Revelation or even of the natural and providential government of the world. In all spheres the Divine processes are gradual, and it would not be reasonable to expect that the Most High should flash upon the eyes of His creatures the full blaze of a complete revelation of Himself without a previous prolonged and careful preparation.

At the same time, if these doctrines are true, we might certainly expect some dim traces or obscure intimations of them in the earlier records of Divine Revelation, and at least we should be sure that in the earlier stages there would be nothing inconsistent with the fuller revelation afterwards to be afforded. We should be sure that these earlier teachings, although themselves incomplete, would yet adapt themselves to the later and fuller disclosures of Divine truth. Like an outline map, they might teach us but little, but that little would be accurate as far as it went, and it would prepare the mind for the more complete revelation afterwards to be given. We might also expect that we should find the revelation brightening onwards from its first dim

twilight to the perfect day of full truth and knowledge. We may say that these expectations have
not been disappointed. The doctrine of the Holy
Trinity, although it is not clearly revealed until
the descent of the Holy Ghost on the Day of
Pentecost, may yet be traced in the very earliest
records of the sacred collections and even in the
beliefs of the heathen. To some it appears to be
reflected in the constitution of the nature of man,
and even in the structure of the material world.

It has been well said that we must not quarrel
with the evidences of the Being of God which
have brought satisfaction to other minds, nor lay
too much stress upon those which approve themselves to our own judgment. In the same way,
we may not deny that there may be validity in
the illustrations of the Holy Trinity which pious
and thoughtful men say they have discovered;
at the same time that we must beware of laying
too great stress upon proofs which are of doubtful
value. It may be that the Creator of all things
intended us to see in the sun, with its central fire
and the light and heat proceeding from it, a
material image of that spiritual Reality by which
all things subsist. The tree with its root, its
trunk, and its branches, may be to many minds
a striking symbol of the same truth.* If we are

*Tertullian, *Adv. Praxeam*, viii.

to see God in everything, we must not quarrel
with those who believe that in these works of
His hands they behold the manifestations of His
Being. Yet it may be safer to employ such
analogies as illustrations of the doctrine and not
to depend upon them as arguments for its truth.
When, again, some of the deepest thinkers of the
Church have seen in the powers of the human
mind a reflection of the Holy Trinity, they not
unreasonably assume that, inasmuch as God has
made man in His own image, these essential dis
tinctions in the Godhead may be expected to be
in some manner and to some extent reproduced
in that created being who was made in His
likeness. For example, S. Augustine finds a
Trinity in the mind—memory, understanding,
and love—and in this trinity beholds the image
of God.* So Leibnitz discovers in man power,
knowledge, and goodness, which in us are partial,
but in God are complete ; † whilst more modern
writers ‡ discover a correspondence between
man's will, thought, and feeling and the three
Persons in the Godhead, the Father, the Son, and
the Holy Ghost. Interesting, however, as the
pursuit of such analogies must be considered, and
helpful as they may be to devout meditation, it

*De Trin. x 14, 10-12.   † Théodicée, Preface.
‡ Delitzsch, Bibl. Psychol. Sec. iv.

may be wiser to abstain from introducing them
as evidences of doctrinal truth.*

It may be well, however, to dwell for a
moment on the well known fact, that the doctrine
of a Trinity in the Godhead has been held and
taught by heathen people, and those too, who, as
far as we know, were uninfluenced by the revelation which was made to the chosen people, the
children of Israel. The instances are somewhat
numerous. It is well known that the Hindoos
believe in a Divine Trinity, whom they designate
by the names of Brahma, Vishnu, and Siva, and
to whom they ascribe attributes and qualities not
unlike those by which the three Persons in
the Holy Trinity, confessed by the Christian
Church, are distinguished.† The most ancient
of the Grecian mythologies, the Orphic, spoke
of the Supreme Being under the threefold character of Light, Counsel, and Life ; and Plato also
taught a doctrine of the Trinity. It is freely
admitted that such facts cannot be regarded as a
proof of the doctrine ; nor are they adduced for

---

*Of the Holy Trinity Itself it has been strikingly observed :
The Father is the Principle, the Fountain of Deity ; the Word
is the Wisdom, the engendered Light ; and the Holy Ghost is
the Bond, the infinite Love of the two first persons. The Holy
Spirit is as the breath of love of the Father and the Son.

†See Professor Max Muller's recently published work on the
" Six Systems of Indian Philosophy."

this purpose. But at least they may be used to rebut the charges of incredibility or improbability.*

When we turn to the contents of the Old and New Testaments, we are on surer ground. As has already been remarked, we must not expect to find any clear testimonies to the doctrine in the Old Testament, whilst at the same time we shall find there many expressions which entirely harmonize with the doctrine taught in the Creeds of the Church.

Thus, on the very first page of the Book of Genesis, we have an account of the creation of the world, which not merely corresponds with later narratives, but which may reasonably suggest to us the doctrine of the Trinity. We cannot, indeed, go so far as to say that the words, "Let us make man in our own image," and other similar expressions can be held to suggest a plurality in the Godhead. Such inferences are manifestly unsafe and may even tend to create a prejudice against the doctrine. But we may reasonably find an indirect testimony to it in the

*"The Socinians may do well to reflect whether that opinion, which was espoused by the deepest thinkers of the ancient world, can be, in itself, so repugnant to natural reason or natural religion as its opponents would have us believe." Heber, Bampton Lectures, Ed. 2, page 122.

language employed to describe the creation, especially when it is compared with the first chapter of the Gospel according to S. John.

In both of these passages we have God the Creator, God creating by His Word, in Genesis implicitly and in S. John explicitly; and in Genesis also the Spirit of God hovering or brooding upon the face of the waters. So again, in the history of the baptism of our Lord in the river Jordan, we are irresistibly drawn to similar reflections. It would perhaps be indefensible to say that this scene proves the doctrine of the Trinity; but it is impossible to deny that it is very impressively suggested and represented by the incidents here recorded. The Son, incarnate to do the will of the Father, stands in the water; the Holy Ghost in the form of a dove hovers over the Son; whilst the voice of the Eternal Father issues from the clouds.

It is not too much to say that the doctrine is at least suggested by the appearance of the three angels to Abraham, when we notice the manner of speech adopted by the mysterious visitants, and the fact that Abraham addresses them either individually or collectively as Jehovah*. As regards the testimony of the New Testament, we

---

*Gen. xviii, 1, 13, 17, 20, 26, 27, 30, 33.

cannot doubt that the doctrine is plainly declared
in the baptismal formula : " Make disciples of all
the nations, baptizing them in the name of
the Father and of the Son and of the Holy
Ghost ;"* and also in the apostolic benediction :
" The grace of the Lord Jesus Christ, and the
love of God and the Communion of the Holy
Ghost be with you all."† But such passages may
be best considered under the special doctrine of
the Holy Ghost.

ii. It is with this subject, the Divinity and Personality of the Holy Spirit that we are here more
immediately concerned ; and to this subject we
must now direct more particular attention. But
first let us ask what we mean when we assert the
proper Godhead of the Holy Spirit. One of our
Creeds declares "The Holy Ghost is God," by which
we assert not merely that He is Divine, but that
He is a Divine Person ; that He is not merely of
one substance with the Father and the Son, but
that He is also personally distinct—not separate,
but distinct—from the Father and the Son. We
assert that He is not a mere attribute, influence,
or energy, but a distinct subsistence ; in perfect
harmony with the other two Persons, but not
identical with them. In short, we declare that,

*S. Matt. xxviii, 19.
†2 Cor. xiii, 14.

while the Father, the Son, and the Holy Ghost are One God, the Holy Ghost is not the Father, or the Son, or a mere influence proceeding from Them.

1. With regard to the Divinity of the Holy Spirit as distinguished from His personality, we do not suppose that there will be any difference of opinion among professing Christians, who are believers in the authority of the New Testament. Indeed it is somewhat difficult to understand how any of those who profess dependence for divine knowledge upon the canonical Scriptures can deny the doctrine of the Holy Trinity We do not mean to say that any individual Christian who might take up his Bible without previous knowledge of these doctrines would at once discover them there. As a matter of fact, we know that it was only after three centuries and many anxious controversies that the Church promulgated these doctrines in the form in which they are now received. But we must hold it for certain that whoever does sincerely, devoutly, and without prejudice search the Scriptures will find sufficient and convincing testimony to the Divinity and Personality of the Holy Ghost, as these doctrines are set forth in the Catholic Creeds.

We shall find, in the Old Testament as well

as the New, names assigned to the Holy
Ghost which belong to God alone; and we shall
find Divine attributes and Divine works distinctly ascribed to Him. If this is true, and if we
further find sufficient testimony to assure us that
He is not a mere influence proceeding from the
Father, but is spoken of as possessed of the same
Personality with the Father and the Son, then
we are justified in asserting that no other theory
of His nature and character will account for
these statements but that which declares Him to
be *very God.*

(1) Remark, in the first place, that the Name
of God or Jehovah is frequently employed inter-
changeably with that of the Holy Spirit. Two
or three examples may suffice. Thus (2 Sam.
xxiii, 2) King David says: " The Spirit of the
Lord spake by me," and in the next verse he
adds, " The God of Israel said." In Isaiah vi. 9,
we read that the voice of Jehovah said to the
prophet, " Go and tell this people, hear ye indeed,
but understand not ;" and S. Paul (Acts xxviii.
25) ascribes those words to the Blessed Spirit ;
" well spake the Holy Ghost by Isaiah the prophet unto your fathers," quoting the words of
Isaiah. So, in the prophetic song of Zacharias
we are told generally that God " spake by the
mouth of His holy prophets," and, in the begin-

ning of the Epistle to the Hebrews, that God of old times spoke to the fathers; whilst S. Peter declares that "holy men of God spake as they were moved by the Holy Ghost."* So, when Ananias was rebuked by S. Peter for his falsehood, the Apostle declared that he had lied " to the Holy Ghost," and again, that he had "not lied unto men, but unto God."†

(2) In the next place, we remark that Divine attributes and actions are ascribed to the Holy Spirit. Thus the author of the Epistle to the Hebrews (ix. 14) speaks of Him as the " Eternal Spirit ;" and in Genesis (i. 2) the work of creation is attributed to Him : " The Spirit of God moved upon the waters." So in Psalm xxxiii. 6, we read, "By the word of the Lord were the heavens made ; and all the host of them by the breath [Spirit] of His mouth." Here the work of creation is ascribed first to the Word of God, who is by S. John identified with the second Person in the Blessed Trinity, and secondly to the Spirit who proceeds from God and the Word. To the same effect we read in Psalm civ. 30 ; " When Thou lettest Thy breath [Spirit] go forth, they shall be made ; and Thou shalt renew the face of the earth."

*St. Luke i. 70 ; Heb. i. 1 ; 2 Pet. i. 21.
†Acts v. 3, 4.

(3) The Divine Spirit is also spoken of as the
worker of miracles. He is the Agent of the
miraculous conception of our Lord. The angel
who appeared to S. Joseph told him concerning
his betrothed, "that which is conceived in her is
of the Holy Ghost." Our Blessed Lord Himself
professed to work miracles by the power of the
Holy Ghost : "If I by the Spirit of God cast out
devils, then is the Kingdom of God come upon
you ;"* and S. Paul, when speaking of the
diversities of gifts which God bestows upon men,
declares : " All these worketh the one and the
same Spirit, dividing to each one severally as
He will."†

These passages, and many others of like character which might be adduced, prove sufficiently
the Divine nature of the Blessed Spirit. On this
aspect of the subject, however, there is the less
need to dwell from the fact that, in some sense,
it is commonly admitted. That which we are
more particularly required to consider, and to
give satisfactory reasons for believing, is the
Personality of the Spirit, a doctrine which is but
loosely held by a considerable number of devout
and reverent Christians.‡ Now, we must repeat,

---

* S. Matthew xii. 28.　†1 Cor. xii. 11.

‡Kahnis (*Die Lehre vom heiligen Geist*) roundly declares that
" modern (*der neuere*) Protestantism has given up the Personality of the Holy Spirit."

this is no unimportant question, but one which strikes at the very foundations of the Catholic faith.

2. The arguments for the Personality of the Holy Spirit are naturally sought in the New Testament, and we may conveniently consider them separately as they occur in the Gospels, in the Acts of the Apostles, and in the Epistles.

(1) The testimony of the Gospels, and especially that of our Blessed Lord, recorded in the Gospels, will demand our first attention. Here we believe the evidence is complete, and will satisfy any one who acknowledges the authority of the Speaker and is willing to take His language in its simple, natural meaning.

Reference has already been made to the incidents connected with the Baptism of our Lord and their significance. Without dwelling longer on this subject and some others which bear a meaning in harmony with it, we would direct attention to the more formal teaching of our Lord with reference to the mission and office of the Holy Spirit, especially as contained in the valedictory address to His disciples, as recorded by S. John, and more particularly in the passages relating to the Comforter.

With regard to the exact meaning of the word, Paraclete, here translated Comforter and elsewhere Advocate, we shall hereafter have something to say. At present we are concerned only with the Personality of the Paraclete. On this point let us consider the force of our Lord's teaching as recorded by S. John, in the fourteenth and sixteenth chapters of his Gospel, "I will pray the Father," He says, "and He shall give you another Comforter, that He may be with you forever, even the Spirit of truth : Whom the world cannot receive; for it beholdeth Him not, neither knoweth Him: ye know Him; for He abideth with you, and shall be in you." Again, "The Comforter, even the Holy Spirit, whom the Father will send in My name, He shall teach you all things, and bring to your remembrance all that I said unto you." Further on in the same address, He says, " It is expedient for you that I go away; for, if I go not away, the Comforter will not come unto you, but if I go I will send Him unto you." And again, "When He,* the Spirit of truth, is come, He shall guide you into all the truth . . . . and He shall declare unto you the things that are to come. He shall glorify me."†

---

*Note here and elsewhere the masculine pronoun *(Ekeinos)*. whereas the Greek for Spirit *(Pneuma)* is neuter.

†S. John xiv. 16 ; xiv. 26 ; xvi. 7, 13, 14.

Such language needs no minute analysis in
order that we may ascertain its meaning. No
words could express more clearly the personality
of the subject concerning whom the testimony is
given. Our Lord contrasts Him with Himself
as " another Paraclete "—a strange manner of
speech if the other Paraclete were a mere influence. Then personal acts and attributes are
assigned to Him : He will teach, He will bring
to remembrance ; when the Lord Jesus departs,
He will come in His place ; and he will guide
into truth, and declare things to come. If
such language does not signify the personality
of the subject, no language could certainly do so.
In the same way, the baptismal formula already
quoted must be held to imply the personality of
the Spirit, seeing that He is connected with the
Father and the Son as co-ordinate with Them. It
would be difficult indeed to imagine that we have,
in these passages, merely strong personifications
of an energy, power, or influence,unless we should
find that such an interpretation was necessitated
by other passages in the New Testament. We
venture to assert that no such passages will be
found.

(2) Let us pass on to the Acts of the Apostles.
Early in the book we come upon the history of
the sin of Ananias, and we find S. Peter charging

him with lying to the Holy Ghost, a strange
expression unless He were a person; and the
meaning is made clearer by the Apostle repeating
the accusation in another form: " Thou hast
not lied unto men, but unto God."*   In the same
book† we read : " As they ministered unto the
Lord, and fasted, the Holy Ghost said, Separate
me Barnabas and Saul for the work whereunto I
have called them." Again, in the letter address-
ed‡ by the first apostolical Council at Jerusalem
to the Church at Antioch, we have the following
words : " It seemed good to the Holy Ghost and
to us to lay upon you no greater burden than
these necessary things." It is needless to comment on such expressions. If they do not convey
to the reader the idea of personality by their own
intrinsic meaning, no amount of argument would
be likely to produce conviction. If we are to
reject such testimony, supported as it is by the
concurrent support of the Church, we must adopt
entirely new methods of dealing with the
Scriptures and with Catholic consent.

(3) The same doctrine is taught and implied
in the apostolical Epistles. We have already
referred to the apostolic benediction in illustration of the doctrine of the Trinity; but it

*Acts v. 3, 4.   †Acts xiii. 2.
‡Acts xv. 28.

is equally clear in support of the personality of
the Holy Spirit. The remarks on the baptismal
formula are here equally applicable. How could
we employ this language: "The grace of our
Lord Jesus Christ, and the love of God, and the
communion of the Holy Ghost be with you all,"
unless the Spirit were co-ordinate with the
Father and the Son. If the Father and the Son
are persons, which no one denies, although different opinions may be held in regard to the
nature of the Son's personality, then surely the
Holy Ghost must be personal also.

But this is by no means a solitary proof of the
doctrine in the epistles. It may be safely said
that there are many passages which necessitate
the assumption of this doctrine, and none which
are at variance with it. Some of the places in
which the Personality of the Spirit is asserted or
implied may be briefly indicated ; it will not be
necessary to dwell upon them at length. Thus
in the Epistle to the Romans (viii. 26) the Spirit
is said to help our infirmity, for "the Spirit Himself maketh intercession for us . . . according
to the will of God." In the first Epistle to the
Corinthians (ii. 11), we read, "The things of God
none knoweth, save the Spirit of God ;" and in
the same epistle (iii. 16), He is said to dwell in us
as in a temple. So, further on (xii.) the Apostle

speaks of the diversities of gifts and the One
Spirit who is the giver ; and in the Epistle to the
Galatians (iv. 6), he tells how " God sent forth
the Spirit of His Son into our hearts, crying
Abba, Father ; " and to go no further, again, in
the Epistle to the Ephesians (iv. 30), he says :
" Grieve not the Holy Spirit of God." When we
take these and other similar passages into consideration, it seems impossible that those who
acknowledge the authority of the witnesses
should hesitate to accept the doctrine.*

iii. To those who appreciate the historical
study of Christian doctrine it will seem of importance to trace the maintenance of the Divinity
and Personality of the Holy Spirit in the teaching
of the Church. Indeed, however plausible our
deduction of a doctrine from Scripture texts may
be, we must not complain if men refuse to accept
our conclusions until we have proved to them
that the Church of the first ages understood the
sacred records in the same sense. Novelties in
doctrine are reasonably suspected ; and if it could
be shown that the opinion which we have maintained was opposed or even unknown in the
times immediately succeeding the days of the

*Reference may here be made to some excellent and con-
vincing remarks in Dr. Stevens's recently published "Theology
of the New Testament," pp. 215 and 245 (T. & T. Clark).

Apostles, this would be a fatal objection to our conclusions.

In tracing the doctrine of the Holy Spirit in the first ages, we may expect similar phenomena to those by which we are confronted in studying the doctrine of the Eternal Word and the God-head of the Lord Jesus Christ. This doctrine was not formulated by the Church until the Council of Nicæa, although it was held implicitly by the Church from the beginning, and the Nicene formula for the first time gave clear and full expression to the teaching. So the doctrine of the Holy Ghost underlay and was involved in the teaching of the Church from the beginning, but was brought to articulate expression in the Creed of Constantinople.*

When we turn to the records of primitive Christianity, we find that, up to the time when heresies arose, rendering necessary a more strict definition of the truth, there was a certain amount of vagueness of expression, which excited neither doubt nor opposition, because it did not conflict with the underlying convictions of the Christian mind. But it may be positively assert-ed that, even before the time of the more exact definition of the doctrine, there are no statements to be found, in authors who represent the mind

*On the primitive faith in the Holy Trinity, see Note A.

of the Church of their age, which are at variance
with those convictions which we have here set
forth as part of the Catholic faith; and, further,
that the references to the Holy Spirit which are
found in the writers of the first three centuries,
are such as either express the doctrine or are in
agreement with it, as it is set forth in the Creed
of Constantinople, or in the *Quicunque Vult*,
known as the Creed of S. Athanasius.

Thus S. Justin Martyr says: "We confess
that we are atheists so far as gods of this kind are
concerned, but not with respect to the most true
God, the Father of righteousness . . .   Both Him
and the Son who came forth from Him—and the
prophetic Spirit, we worship and adore, knowing
them in reason and truth.*

To a similar effect Athenagoras speaks in his
Plea for Christians.†   "Who would not marvel,"
he asks, "to hear men call us atheists, although
we speak of God the Father, and God the Son,
and the Holy Ghost, and set forth at once their
power in unity and their distinction in order."

In the *Martyrdom of Polycarp*, a document
belonging to the first half of the second century,
we find the following: "We wish you, brethren,
all happiness, while you walk according to the

---

* *Apolog.* i. 6.
† *Leg.* 10, cf. 12 and 24.

doctrine of the Gospel of Jesus Christ, with whom
be glory to God the Father and the Holy Spirit ;"
and in the *Martyrdom of Ignatius,* somewhat
later, the concluding words are as follows : " In
Christ Jesus our Lord, by Whom and with Whom,
be glory and power to the Father, with the Holy
Spirit for evermore.   Amen."

S. Irenæus teaches distinctly the Godhead of
the Holy Ghost and His personal distinction from
the Father and the Son. " In all and through
all," he says, " there is one God, the Father ; and
one Word, the Son ; and one Spirit; and to all
who believe in Him one Salvation."*

By the time of Tertullian the heresy of Patri-
passianism, advocated by Praxeas, the forerunner
of Sabellius, had arisen ; and Tertullian set himself in opposition to this error.   It has been said
that his language is somewhat uncertain ; but a
closer examination of his statements will satisfy
us that this effect is produced by his eagerness
to confute some of the other rising errors of his
day.   It is certain that he did in fact hold that
which was subsequently promulgated as the
Catholic doctrine, " As if," he says, " in this
way also One were not All, since all are of One,
namely by unity of substance ; and nevertheless

Adv. Hær. iv, 20, 1.

the mystery of the dispensation (*Oikonomias*) is preserved, which distributes the Unity into a Trinity, placing the Three in order, the Father and the Son and the Holy Spirit. They are three, however, not in condition but in degree; not in substance but in form; not in power but in aspect; yet of one substance and of one condition, and of one power, inasmuch as God is One." That Tertullian did not mean for a moment to deny the distinct personality is clear from what he says of Praxeas. He declares that this heretic by his teaching "had put the Paraclete to flight, and had crucified the Father."*

If the doctrine of the Personality of the Holy Spirit was assailed by Praxeas and Noëtus, and afterwards by Sabellius, the Divinity of the Spirit was assailed by Macedonius, following in the footsteps of Arius in his denial of the Godhead of Christ. Up to the time of the Council of Nicæa little attention had been paid to heresies touching the Third Person of the Holy Trinity; and the Creed which was promulgated at this Council, after carefully defining the doctrine concerning the God-man, came to an abrupt close, with the words: "And in the Holy Ghost."

*Adv. Praxeam, ii.

About a quarter of a century later, however, Macedonius ascended the patriarchal throne of Constantinople (A.D. 351), and, while asserting the Nicene doctrine of the Second Person, he began to promulgate a heresy which denied the true Godhead of the Holy Spirit, declaring Him to be a mere creature, although more perfect than other creatures. Macedonius died disgraced A.D. 361, but a considerable sect arose, known as Macedonians or Pneumatomachi, by whom his opinions were disseminated. They were condemned by the Council of Constantinople (A.D. 381), which completed the Nicene Creed by bringing it into the form in which we now possess it, with the exception of the words: "And the Son" (*filioque*). The part on the Holy Spirit ran as follows : "And in the Holy Ghost, the Lord,* the Life-giver, proceeding from the Father, who with the Father and the Son is worshipped and glorified, who spake by the prophets.'

It can hardly be said that the heresy was thus extinguished, but it never afterwards had any real influence in the Church ; and this form of error was either unknown or insignificant until the time of the Socini, the founders of modern

---

*The word (like that for Life-giver) in the Greek is an adjective, *to kurion*.

Unitarianism in the sixteenth century. Even if
Unitarianism had retained its earlier form,
assigning a certain authority to the Sacred
Scriptures and recognizing a supernatural element in the mission and work of the Lord
Jesus Christ, its doctrines could hardly claim to
be considered as a form of the Christian faith.
In its present form of simple Deism, it hardly
pretends to any specifically Christian elements.
The Bible is merely a book, doubtless one of the
best, or even the very best of books, of sacred
literature, and Jesus Christ is one of the greatest,
or even the greatest of religious teachers, but
having no more authority over the life of man
than the inner sense or conscience is willing to
recognize.

iv. There is, however, one other point which
demands some notice at our hands, that of the
procession of the Holy Spirit from the Godhead,
and the later form of the doctrine, in which He
is said to proceed from the Father *and the Son.*
With regard to the procession of the Holy Spirit
from the Father, no controversy has arisen. As
the Son is said to be *begotten* of the Father, so the
Holy Spirit is declared (S. John xv. 26) to be
" the Spirit of truth, which *proceedeth* from the
Father "; and again (xiv. 26) " Whom the
Father will send in My Name." Doubtless there

is a reason for this distinction, even if we can only guess at it or partly discern it. It must be noted, however, that this generation and this procession is eternal, and not merely economic, or relative to the salvation of mankind; for this would be to abandon the doctrine of the proper Godhead of the Son and of the Holy Spirit.

The Council of Ephesus, in adopting the Creed of Constantinople, decreed that no other should be used, and it has been questioned whether this did not forbid any additions to the Creed. Such power, however, no council could possess; and, in any case, it was not long before it became customary with the Latin theologians to speak of the procession of the Spirit from the Father *and the Son*. Such expressions we find in the writings of S. Ambrose, S. Augustine, and S. Leo. It is perhaps to be regretted that the phrase became current in the Western Church without the consent of the Orientals. It was introduced into the Creed of the first Synod of Toledo (A.D. 447), and made part of the Nicene or Constantinopolitan Creed at the Third Synod of Toledo (A.D. 589). For a time the addition was resisted at Rome, but finally it was taken into the Creed of the Western Church. The controversy is more verbal than real. The Greeks would accept the formula, " proceeding from the

Father through the Son"; and this would give
essentially the same meaning. The Scripture
testimony may certainly be regarded as estab-
lishing the doctrine of the double procession.
It is true, our Lord says, that the Spirit of truth
proceedeth from the Father, and that He will
pray the Father to send another Comforter; but
He also says, "Whom I will send unto you from
the Father," and moreover the Holy Ghost is
called the "Spirit of the Son" and the "Spirit
of Christ," as plainly as He is declared to be the
"Spirit of the Father," or the "Spirit of God."
While, therefore, it is to be regretted that a
difference has here arisen between the East and
the West, there is no real disagreement in
regard to essential doctrine.

Here then we take our stand respecting the
doctrine of the Holy Spirit, as part of the
Catholic Faith. "We worship one God in
Trinity, and Trinity in Unity," confessing that
"the Father is God, the Son is God, and the
Holy Ghost is God; and yet they are not three
Gods, but one God." This is the teaching of the
New Testament and the faith of the Church of
Christ. It is the faith into which we were bap-
tized, which is taught in our churches, and
which will be confessed at our graves. It is the
faith in which we live and in which we hope to

die; which will be our strength and our shield
in prosperity and adversity, in health and in
sickness, in life and in death.

It is indeed a doctrine of vital importance. It
is no mere open question respecting which men
may hold harmlessly differences of opinion. It
is an essential part of the faith of the Catholic
Church. It affects our relation to Christian
truth in many ways. How can we understand
aright the nature of the Church of Christ itself,
if we are ignorant of Him who dwells in the
Church as a living temple; who is the very life
of the mystical Body of Christ? How can we
know the nature, significance or effect of the
Sacraments, if we know not Him from whom
they derive their life and their power? Or how
shall our spiritual life be duly fostered and
strengthened if we are in error concerning the
Giver of life, who is with us to lead us into all
truth, and is the Author of every grace and of
every gift?

LECTURE II.

THE PROMISE OF THE FATHER.

The Gift of the Holy Ghost at Pentecost not a larger effusion, but a distinct event, a personal revelation. Analogy of the Gift of the Eternal Son. This gift predicted and prepared for. I. The Old Testament. Old Testament prophecies. Interpreted by apostles and inspired writers. II. The New Testament. Holy Ghost not given until a certain moment. S. John vii, 39—S. John xvi, 7. 1. The greatness of this gift. 2. Its connexion with the work of Christ.—(1) Christ revealed truth of God and man ; (2) Offered a Sacrifice ; (3) Assumed His throne of intercession and government. 3. Completeness of divine revelation. Our responsibility and our privileges.

IT is a truth almost self-evident and, indeed, generally recognized, that we understand the parts of a system only as we perceive their relation to the whole. The application of this general principle to the Catholic faith will be questioned only by those who have gone but a little way in the study of theology.

It is not too much to say that the doctrine of the Holy Spirit has been, in some of its details at least, misunderstood or imperfectly appreciated from the failure to estimate its place in the divine economy. It is the same with all truths each forms a whole, and only in the light of the whole do the parts stand out clearly in the fullness of their meaning. So it is with the work of Christ and its preparations. On the one hand the Hebrew economy would be obscure, unmeaning, contradictory, if we did not know that it was a preparation for the work of the Redeemer, the Prophet, Priest, and King of humanity—a preparation rendered necessary by the moral and intellectual condition of mankind. On the other hand, the work of Christ for man's salvation has much light shed upon it by the Hebrew system carefully and devoutly studied. In the same way, the work of the Divine Spirit is inseparably connected with the whole antecedent revelation of God, in Nature, in Providence, in the Law and the Prophets, and in Christ.

When we survey the whole history of God's dealings with men we become conscious of an end towards which everything is tending—

> ' One far-off event
> To which the whole creation moves."

This end is the perfection of God's highest work, the realization of the divine idea of the human race, the final establishment of the Kingdom of God. This is the end which is proclaimed in the final note of triumph which celebrates the consummation of all things : " The

kingdom of the world is become our Lord's and
His Christ's "; and again, "The Lord our God,
the Almighty, reigneth." *

A moment's consideration will satisfy us that
the whole divine process can be made intelligible only as it is regarded in reference to this
end.   Thus S. John the Baptist and our Blessed
Lord alike began their public ministry with the
announcement : " The Kingdom of Heaven is at
hand;" and after the descent of the Holy Ghost the
apostles went forth "preaching good tidings concerning the Kingdom of God." †   The establishment of this kingdom was equally, although in
different ways, the work of the Divine Son and
the Divine Spirit, and, if the work of Christ was
the necessary preparation for that of the Holy
Ghost, equally was the work of the Redeemer
prepared for by the long process of the antecedent revelation.

Now, it is with the actual gift of the Holy
Spirit, the fulfilment of that great "promise of
the Father," that we have specially to do at
present.   And we desire to note at once that the
coming of the Holy Ghost was a gift of God to
man as definite and as clearly referred to a
moment in history as the Advent of the Word

*Rev. xi. 15 ; xix. 6.
†Acts viii. 12.

made flesh when he came to visit mankind " in great humility." We are accustomed to hear men speak of the Gift of Pentecost, as though it were one of many outpourings of the Spirit of God, a special effusion indeed, yet differing only in degree, but not in kind, from many other such events. We are persuaded that a more careful examination of the testimonies on the subject in the New Testament will satisfy us that this is a statement which has only a measure of truth, and which overlooks the important fact that the Advent of the Holy Ghost on Pentecost was a unique event in the history of the world. It was an event that was prepared for through many ages, and which was attended by far-reaching consequences for many ages, consequences which are being realized now, and will be realized in Eternity. But the event itself took place at a definite moment, at the Feast of Pentecost in Jerusalem, just as the birth of the Son of God took place at a certain moment in Bethlehem.

Indeed it would not be easy to gain a clearer conception of the coming of the Spirit than by pointing out its correspondence with that of the Son. Both were in the world always, as Divine persons, and both were personally revealed at a given moment in the history of the world. So it was with the Eternal Word. "He was in the world, and the world was made by Him." "In Him was life, and the life was the light of men . . . even the light that lighteth every man coming into the world."* But all this time He was not personally revealed. It was only when "the Word became Flesh, and dwelt among us . . . full of grace and truth";† it was when He was made flesh and was born of a woman, "and we beheld His glory," that He was revealed personally, and as distinct from the Father, God and "with God." So, in the same manner, the Divine Spirit was always in the world as the Spirit of God, but it was not until the Day of Pentecost that He was personally revealed.

Enough has already been said to assure us that due preparation would be made for this "unspeakable Gift" as for that of the Incarnate Word; and it is of interest—we might say it is indispensable—that we should trace this preparation in the Old Testament and in the history of the work of Christ recorded in the Gospels.

There was a sense, as has been hinted, in which the Holy Spirit was known under the

* S. John i. 10, 4, 9.
† S. John i. 14.

earlier dispensation. He was the active Agent
in creation. He is also acknowledged as, in
some sense, the Sanctifier of men. "Take not
Thy Holy Spirit from me," is the prayer of the
penitent psalmist; and again, "Uphold me with
Thy free Spirit."* These and other similar
passages are in perfect harmony with what has
already been said of the presence of the Divine
Spirit in earlier times. But we find very clear
intimations in the Old Testament of a time in
the future in which the Spirit was to be given
as He had not been given before; and this intimation assumes a clearness of form in the words
of our Lord which leaves no doubt as to the
meaning of the promise.

i. But first let us notice some of the passages
in the Old Testament which refer to the Holy
Spirit, and some which are declared by the
speakers and writers in the New Testament to
have reference to the coming of the Holy Spirit
at Pentecost.

And here we are met by the objection that we
are bringing into the Old Testament Scriptures
meanings of which their writers had no conception; and further an attempt is made to eliminate the whole predictive element from Old

---

*Psalm li. 11, 12.

Testament prophecy, and to assign to it only a moral and spiritual significance.

It would be impossible, in this place, to discuss so large a subject at length; but some general remarks may be permitted. In the first place, we are not here arguing the supernatural character of the Christian religion. We are assuming that Jesus Christ is the Son of God. Now, if this is the truth, if Christ is God manifest in the flesh, it is most reasonable that so great an event should be prepared for. If this miracle is true, almost any antecedent miracle may be expected, and should not be rejected, unless it comes to us inadequately certified. So much for the probability of the case.

Again, that words, spoken by prophets under Divine inspiration, should contain within themselves a meaning not intelligible to those by whom they were promulgated, is not merely reasonable, but must seem almost necessary ; and S. Peter tells us,* in very striking language, that this was the case. He says the prophets who testified beforehand the sufferings and glories of Christ, searched into the meaning of their predictions, "to whom it was revealed that not unto themselves, but unto you, did they minister these things."

*I. S. Peter i. 10-12.

Two things we may set down as our warrant for the use we make of the Old Testament prophecy. These writings themselves point us forward to a period in the future in which their contents should be realized ; and, moreover, they are interpreted by apostles and canonical writers as referring to the times of the Messiah and the establishment and extension of the Christian Church.

1. Passing over a number of references to the agency of the Spirit, some of which will be noticed in another connection, we select one text from the second chapter of the Book of the Prophet Joel, which is of primary importance, not only because its language is most explicit, but especially because it is expounded by S. Peter, in his discourse on the Day of Pentecost itself, as being a prediction of the great event of that day.

The portion quoted by S. Peter as referring to the Christian Pentecost is contained in verses 28 to 32, and more particularly with reference to the Holy Spirit, in verses 28 and 29 ; and they are introduced by the statement :* "This is that which hath been spoken by the Prophet Joel." With regard to the section preceding,

* Acts ii. 16

we shall be strongly tempted to see here fore-
casts of the Kingdom of Christ.

As, however, there is great variety in the
interpretation of the passage, it would be
neither modest nor wise to speak confidently as
to the precise reference intended. But there is
one point on which commentators seem to be
substantially agreed; that, whilst there may be
a prediction here relating to the more immediate history of Israel, the words are intended
to direct our minds onwards to a more perfect
consummation of the Divine purpose in the
Kingdom of the Messiah. Such an idea would
correspond well with the promise of joy and
gladness, the removal of all the evils brought
upon the chosen people by their own sinfulness,
and the bestowal of all spiritual blessing.

And this reference to the Kingdom of the
Messiah is rendered more probable by its connection with the gift of the Holy Spirit; and on
this point we have the distinct testimony of S.
Peter. S. Luke is quite clear in his account.*
The people, he says, "were all amazed and
were perplexed," and Peter told them ; "This is
that which hath been spoken by the Prophet
Joel: And it shall be in the last days, saith God,

*Acts ii. 14-18.

I will pour forth of My Spirit upon all flesh; and your sons and your daughters shall prophesy, and your young men shall see visions, and your old men shall dream dreams; yea, and on my servants and on my handmaidens in those days will I pour forth of My Spirit." There the gift of the Holy Spirit is spoken of as a kind of consummation of God's mercies to sinful men, and a blessing which is to be extended, not to Israel alone, but to all flesh.

Another passage, often quoted as prophetic of the gift of the Holy Spirit in connection with the work of Christ, is Haggai ii. 4-7. There can be no doubt, we think, that in their primary meaning these words refer to the restoration of the chosen people to their own land, after the lengthened captivity in Babylon. A comparison is instituted between this emancipation and the deliverance in earlier days from the bondage of Egypt; "According to the word that I covenanted with you when ye came out of Egypt, and My Spirit abode with you, fear ye not." In the revised translation the reference to the history of Israel is even stronger. Yet the language which follows seems to point to something greater to come: "It is a little while, and I will shake the heavens, and the earth, and the sea, and the dry land; and I will shake all nations, and the desirable things (the Desire, A.V.) of all nations shall come, and I will fill this house with glory, saith the Lord of hosts."

Certainly there would seem to be more here than a mere national deliverance ; and further, the deliverances of Israel are recognized as typical of the salvation of mankind from a darker Egypt, from a more grinding servitude than that of Babylon. When, therefore, we find that the Fathers of the Church* who comment upon this passage are practically unanimous in recognizing here the promise of the Holy Spirit, we may perhaps condemn our own lack of Christian sympathy, rather than the critical faculty of those who find more of the New Testament in the Old than we do.

But however we may judge of the passage quoted from Haggai, those at least who admit the authority of the Gospel according to S. John will not call in question the prophetic signifi- cance of the words of Zechariah (xii. 10) : "I will pour upon the house of David, and upon the inhabitants of Jerusalem, the Spirit of grace and of supplication ; and they shall look upon Me whom they have pierced ; and they shall mourn for Him as one that is in bitterness for his first-

---

*Among these are Athanasius, Cyril of Jerusalem, Gregory of Nyssa, Theodoret, and Jerome.

born." When we follow the leading of S. John (xix. 37) and refer this passage to the work of Christ and of the Holy Spirit, we have no thought of denying that it had a primary application to Israel. But we must hold that the blessings here described as being poured upon the house of David and the inhabitants of Jerusalem had a more extensive reference; and this is confirmed by the contents of the following chapter, in which we read that "in that day there shall be a fountain opened to the house of David and to the inhabitants of Jerusalem, for sin and for uncleanness."

The Holy Spirit is here set forth, not so much as the consequence of the work of the Son. He is represented as applying the work of Christ to the hearts and consciences of men. When He is poured forth upon those who have contemplated the death of the Messiah, they will be brought to know that they have themselves crucified the Son of God; and they will mourn because they have pierced him. It is an anticipation of the words of Jesus, in reference to the advent of the Paraclete: "He, when He is come, will convict the world in respect of sin, and of righteousness, and of judgment." *

* S. John xvi. 8.

2. We must now refer to a class of passages which, more or less clearly, bring out not merely the fact of the future gift of the Holy Spirit, but the nature of the special work which He is destined to perform. The great work of the Holy Spirit is the recreation of the world and of man, the regeneration and sanctification of the human race in Christ, and the harmonious development and completion of the Church of God.

Thus the Psalmist declares: "Thou sendest forth Thy Spirit, they are created; and Thou renewest the face of the earth." * The striking prophecy in the eleventh chapter of the Book of the Prophet Isaiah † describes at some length the process by which the change is effected through the agency of Him who is the stem and branch of Jesse, by the power of the sevenfold Spirit: "There shall come forth a shoot out of the stock of Jesse, and a branch out of his roots shall bear fruit; and the Spirit of the Lord shall rest upon him . . . and his delight shall be in the fear of the Lord; . . . with righteousness shall He judge the poor, and reprove with equity for the meek of the earth. . .; and righteousness shall be the girdle of His loins, and faithfulness the girdle of His reins. . . They shall not hurt

* Psalm civ. 30.   † Isaiah xi. 1-9.

nor destroy in all My holy mountain ; for the earth shall be full of the knowledge of the Lord, as the waters cover the sea."

We have certainly no desire to set aside the application of such language to the history of Israel and the divine deliverances and blessings of which the chosen people were the object. The fortunes of the Israelites were bound up with those of the house of David, to whom Jehovah had promised the sovereignty over His people ; and the prophetic language of Isaiah had a partial fulfilment in the restoration of the people to the land of promise. But we must never forget that Israel had a typical and prophetic character, representing and preparing for the Kingdom of God, to be manifested in the fullness of time ; and that the rulers of Israel were the types of that ideal King who was appointed to rule the world in righteousness, and bring all men to the knowledge and obedience of Jehovah.

It is not merely that the passage before us has no adequate fulfilment in the history of Israel It could not be that, under any such order in its most perfect realization, the whole earth should be full of the knowledge of the Lord. But we find in these words a very striking anticipation of the work of the Saviour Christ and of the Holy Spirit of God, in accomplishing the redemp-

tion and sanctification of mankind. Our Lord
is described as "a shoot out of the stock of
Jesse," humble and lowly, springing out of the
earth, yet endued with life and power, having
the Spirit of the Lord resting upon Him ; and in
this Spirit of seven gifts we recognize of necessity the third Person in the blessed Trinity.
Even rationalistic commentators have recognized
a Messianic reference in this prophecy, and of
what other spirit could such things be spoken ?
And further, it could only be by the action of
this mighty Spirit that all discord and enmity
could be banished from the earth, and the
knowledge and fear of God universally prevail.
If Christ assumed His place as universal sove-
reign when He sat down on the right hand of
God, He put forth His great power and reigned
effectually when the Holy Ghost came down
from heaven to earth on the Day of Pentecost.

No less striking is the language employed by
the Prophet Ezekiel to describe the work of the
Holy Spirit * : "I will sanctify My great name,
which hath been profaned among the nations
. . . And I will sprinkle clean water upon you,
and ye shall be clean : from all your filthiness
and from all your idols will I cleanse you. A
new heart also will I give you, and a new spirit

* Ezekiel xxxvi. 23.27.

will I put within you ; and I will take away the stony heart out of your flesh, and I will give you a heart of flesh. And I will put My Spirit within you, and cause you to walk in My statutes, and ye shall keep My judgments and do them. And ye shall dwell in the land that I gave to your fathers ; and ye shall be My people and I will be your God."

Here, again, we have predictions which found a partial fulfilment in the fact that the Jews, after the captivity, did not again fall into the sin of idolatry. Some, too, have found an allusion to the cleansing fountain which flows from the wounded side of the Lamb of God, although, in view of what follows, the reference is more probably to the working of the Divine Spirit, whose agency is frequently compared to that of water. But at least the latter part of the prophecy finds its most natural and complete fulfilment in the gift of Pentecost, the descent of the Holy Spirit.

On this point the Christian Church seems to have entertained no doubt ; and perhaps we may say that this view is confirmed by a passage from the Prophet Jeremiah, as interpreted in the Epistle to the Hebrews.* We quote from

---

* Jeremiah xxxi. 31-34 ; Hebrews viii. 8-13.

the New Testament: "Behold, the days come,
saith the Lord, that I will make a new covenant with the house of Israel, and with the
house of Judah. . . For this is the covenant
that I will make with the house of Israel after
those days, saith the Lord; I will put My laws
into their mind, and on their heart also will I
write them; and I will be to them a God, and
they shall be to Me a people." These words, the
writer tells us, find their fulfilment in the new
and better covenant, of which Christ is the
Mediator, and in the application of which the
Holy Spirit is the living power.

Before leaving the sphere of Old Testament
prophecy, let us turn again to the book of the
Prophet Ezekiel,* and first to the vision of the
valley full of dry bones. "Behold," saith the
Lord, "I will cause breath to enter into you, and
ye shall live;" and "the breath came into them
and they lived, and stood up upon their feet."
Here, if we cannot claim to find a direct reference to the Gift of Pentecost, there is a clear
allusion to the regenerating power of the Holy
Spirit. So, in a later passage of the same Prophet,† streams of water are represented as coming
forth from the altar, an almost literal prediction of

*Ezekiel xlvii. 1, 2.
† Ezekiel xxxvii. 1-14.

that "river of water of life, bright as crystal,
proceeding out of the throne of God and of the
Lamb,"* representing the procession of the Holy
Ghost, and the coming of this Gift as depending
upon the sacrifice of Christ.

No less striking is the similar representation
in the Prophet Zechariah : † "It shall come to
pass in that day that living waters shall go out
from Jerusalem ; half of them toward the eastern
sea, and half of them toward the western sea."—
a very striking image of the fact and the consequences of the Gift of the Holy Ghost, whose
manifestations began at Jerusalem, and went
forth from thence to regenerate all the nations of
the earth.

We have not sought to press into the service of
this doctrine every available passage and allusion. It may be indeed that some will hesitate
to follow us in our application of all of these
prophecies to the great event of Pentecost. Yet
when we remember the awful import of the
Coming of the Holy Ghost, its preparations, its
accompaniments, and its consequences, even if
we concede that there may, in these passages,
be allusions to the working of the Divine Spirit
in the earlier dispensation—which we are, in no
way, concerned to deny—we shall probably con-

*Rev. xxii, 1.   †Zech. xiv, 8.

clude that, in the mind of Him by whom these
holy men of old were inspired, there was a pro-
spective reference to that which is the culmin-
ating point of the whole process of Divine
revelation, the Gift of the Holy Spirit.

To many it may seem that we have neglected
passages in the Old Testament in which they
discover allusions to His work: and we find
no fault with those who may meet with such
testimonies in many parts of the earlier records.*
Undoubtedly the sacrificial ordinances will often
bring such suggestions to the devout mind. For
our purpose, however, it has sufficed to have
pointed out that the work of the Spirit, no less
than that of the Son, was provided and prepared
for under the old covenant, that, in the Old
Testament as well as in the New, the work of our
Lord and that of the Holy Spirit are inseparable;
and that the same work, that of cleansing, regenerating, renewing, which is attributed to Him
in the New Testament, is ascribed to Him in the
Old.

This work of the Holy Spirit, then, was no less
a part of the plan and purpose of the Most High
for the salvation of mankind than the work of
our Lord Jesus Christ Himself. The Day of

---

*It was said that Cocceius found Christ everywhere in the
Old Testament and Grotius found Him nowhere. We should
incline to say, "Malo errare cum Cocceio."

Pentecost was as necessary to the Church and to the world as Christmas Day. If man needed to know God manifest in the flesh, the High Priest of Humanity, he no less needed the presence of Him who dwells in the body of the Church, and in the heart of the Christian, to illuminate, to purify, to enliven, to strengthen, and to comfort; to lead into all truth in thought and word and deed.

In regard to these points we are not left to the probable inferences derivable from prophecy or even to the moral certainty which we may gain from typical or symbolical teaching. We have the plain and explicit teaching of the Lord Jesus, when He was preparing His disciples for His own departure and for the coming of the Paraclete. In that teaching He sets forth the supreme importance of the Advent of the Spirit, its dependence upon the completion of His own appointed work, as well as some leading features of the ministry of the Paraclete. These points demand the most careful attention, if we would rightly understand this doctrine, as far as that may be possible for us in our present condition.

In regard to the greatness of the work of the Paraclete, it would not be easy to state it in stronger terms than those employed by our Lord:*

*S. John xvi. 7.

"It is expedient for you that I go away; for if I go not away, the Comforter will not come unto you; but, if I go, I will send Him unto you." Now, here once more, let us note distinctly how it is implied in these words that there is a sense in which the Holy Spirit is not yet present, a sense in which He has yet to come. And this is clearly set forth by S. John in another place,* when commenting upon our Lord's promise of the Spirit, given at an earlier period: "This spake He of the Spirit which they that believe on Him were to receive: for the Spirit was not yet given because Jesus was not yet glorified." This is quite explicit, and we cannot doubt as to the meaning of it. In the words of Augustine, He was now to come no longer as a transient Visitor, but as an eternal inhabitant. The saints had not been without experience of the graces of the Divine Spirit, but he had not hitherto been revealed as a Person. In that sense He was not yet given.

The greatness of that gift is set forth in the strongest language by our Lord, language which surprised His disciples by its strength, for it declares that there would be a special advantage to them in losing the personal, physical presence of their Master, since that was the condition of the presence of the "other Ad-

*S. John vii. 39.

vocate," the Holy Spirit. The significance of this promise, it is hoped, will come out in subsequent lectures; but it may be proper to dwell for a moment on its general importance at this point.

1. Let us remember that this work of Divine grace was a work of transformation, in which man was to be prepared for the fellowship of God. The work of Jesus Christ was essential to this end. It may still be called the central work of salvation, since it is Jesus whom we call Saviour, and not the Holy Ghost, although He too may be said to save us; and we are called Christians in token of our faith in Christ as our Lord. Yet the work of Christ, great and glorious as it was, needed to be completed by another Paraclete. If it was necessary for us that God should be brought down to earth, to live there as man, no less did we need to have God come and dwell within us. If we needed that Christ should rule us, as second Adam, as greater David, from His exalted throne, no less did we need that the word of Christ should be made a living power in mind, heart and will; that God should not only speak to our ears and our intelligence, but also that He should enter within us and search the thoughts of our hearts and change our affections and illuminate our spiritual perceptions and guide our wills "It is expedient for you," says our Lord,

that this change should take place in your circumstances, in your privileges and experiences.

2. And then He points out that there was an
inseparable connexion between His own work
and that of the Holy Spirit. "If I go not away,
the Comforter will not come unto you; but if I
go, I will send Him unto you." To the same
general effect S. John had said : "The Spirit was
not yet given, because Jesus was not yet glorified."

Now, here there are two things to be noted. On
the one hand we must beware of laying down
conditions as though we had a right to pre-
scribe to the Almighty how He must effect His
own purposes. But, when he declares that there
is a necessity, then we are bound to accept His
word, and reverently enquire into its meaning.
In that case, the necessity is none of our making:
we are not imposing conditions upon the Most
High. It is He whose supreme wisdom prescribes
to His own will : the necessity is internal. Yet,
on the other hand, our Blessed Lord here does
tell us that there is some kind of necessary con.
nexion between the fulfilling of His own work
and the coming of the Holy Spirit, and we may
humbly and reverently inquire into the character
of that connexion.

(1) In what way, then, may we consider that

the work of Christ was a preparation, and even
a necessary preparation for the coming of the
Holy Spirit? Various answers may be given to
such a question. In the first place, it is of primary importance that men should obtain light,
knowledge; that they should know something of
the nature of God, and of the nature of man.
Such knowledge would be a necessary preliminary to any beneficial influence on the character. A mere sentiment, separated from enlightened judgment, could end only in hazy
mysticism or superstitions. We have many
examples of this kind among men now living
upon the earth; and it would hardly have been
different in the case (if we could imagine the
case) of men subjected to the best of all influences—to the influence of the Spirit of God,
if there had been no basis of truth and
knowledge to work upon. Such a foundation,
however, was laid in the ministry of Him who
could say, "I am the way and the truth and the
life," and, "He that hath seen Me hath seen the
Father."

(2) Another prerequisite in order to the meet-
ing of God and man is the sacrifice of Christ by
which those who were far off were brought nigh.
Here is the deep mystery of the atonement which
we cannot understand in all its extent, but which

yet responds to the need of man and the demand
of God. This at least we know that in every
nation and in all ages men have sought reconciliation with God through sacrifice; and that
they have sought it in vain. "For," says the
writer of the Epistle to the Hebrews,* "it is impossible that the blood of bulls and goats should
take away sins," but not like theirs is the power
of the blood of Christ. "Having, therefore,
brethren, boldness to enter into the holy place
by the blood of Jesus," we can "draw near with
a true heart, in fullness of faith," knowing that
there remains now no obstacle to freedom of
communion between the soul and God.

(3.) And perhaps we may say that there is one
other thought in regard to the connexion between
the work of the Redeemer and that of the Sanctifier; that, namely, which is indicated by S.
John when he says that the Spirit was not given
because Jesus was not glorified. For we are
here reminded of the assumption of power by the
Second Adam, when he rose up from earth to
heaven, and sat down at the right hand of God.
He had earned the right to be there, not merely
with the glory which He had with the Father
before the world began, but with a glory which
He had won for humanity, and which He could

*Heb. x, 4, 19.

now claim for the whole race of man. When
He ascended up on high, leading captivity cap-
tive, He could then claim, and receive gifts for
men, that the Lord God might dwell among
them. Here, then, we find the consummation of
the thought, " if I go away, I will send Him unto
you." It was in prospect of the bestowal of this
great gift, that He charged His disciples not to
depart from Jerusalem, but to wait for the
promise of the Father; and that promise was
fulfilled when the Holy Ghost, on the Day of
Pentecost, came down from heaven to dwell with
men upon the earth.

3. Well may we, as we meditate upon the
wonders of divine grace, cry out: "Thanks be
unto God for His unspeakable gift;" for it is the
gift of Himself; and there is nothing more that
even He could give. Well may He ask, and
bid us consider the question : "What could have
been done more to My vineyard that I have not
done in it?" On the Day of Pentecost He had
done all and given all that there was to give. He
had given Himself.

Yet, let it be noted, it is not meant that God
has done all that He has purposed to do in the
world and among men. It would be truer to say
that the work had only been begun than to say
that it has been ended. Even in the knowledge of

Divine truth all had not been reached at a
stroke. The Paraclete was, indeed, to lead them
into all the truth, but this was to be done as they
were able to receive it. Nearly three hundred
years were to elapse before the doctrine of the
Incarnate Word was defined with exactness.
Another half century had to pass before the
Church was guarded against error touching the
Person of the Holy Ghost. Many lessons of
unspeakable value have been communicated to
the Church during the ages that have gone by;
and those who have ears to hear may listen and
learn still from the oracles of the living God
interpreted by the Spirit of Truth. Yea, we are
sure the time will never come when the Voice
of the Spirit shall be silent and the members of
Christ shall have no more to learn concerning
the mysteries of the Kingdom.

Yet we may truly say that the Revelation of
God in this dispensation is complete—completed
in the gift of the Holy Ghost. What may be in
store for the Church and the world, when the Son
of man shall come in the glory of His Father
with all His holy angels, we cannot tell, or we
can tell it but imperfectly, for that future we
see only through a glass darkly; but until then
there will be no fresh revelation of God and no
new gift of His grace. God has already done

all that needs to be done for us, in order that we may prepare to meet our Lord. What can we render unto Him for all His benefits, or how can we fitly acknowledge His boundless love, His unspeakable gift?

How great, how tremendous is our responsibility! If He, who has done so much for His vineyard, should come seeking fruit, what has He not a right to expect? If He should find us scorning or neglecting the gracious provision which He has made, with what terrible force will that dread warning apply: "Of how much sorer punishment, think ye, shall he be judged worthy, who hath trodden under foot the Son of God, and hath counted the Blood of the Covenant, wherewith he was sanctified, an unholy thing, and hath done despite unto the Spirit of grace?"*

And yet, needful as such reflections may sometimes be, it is not with thoughts like these that we would bring to a close our meditations upon such a subject. Rather shall we rejoice and give thanks for the grace which has armed us so completely for fighting the good fight of faith which enables us to say: "I can do all things in Him that strengtheneth me."† Great and powerful indeed are the enemies who are arrayed

*Heb. x. 29.   †Phil. iv. 13.

against us. "Our wrestling is not against flesh
and blood, but against the principalities, against
the powers."*   But we do not fight in our own
strength: "Greater is He that is in you than he
that is in the world."†   In this faith we can
stand, neither fainting nor fearing. In this faith
we can "take up the whole armor of God that
we may be able to withstand in the evil day, and,
having done all, to stand."‡

*Ephes. vi. 12.   †S. John iv. 4.   ‡Ephes. vi. 13.

LECTURE III.

THE FASHIONER OF THE SECOND ADAM.

The Fall—Recovery—The Means : The God Man. How Prepared.
I. The Second Adam, source of new life to man. 1. The Ideal
man. 2. The God man. II. Agent in preparing Second Adam
the Holy Spirit. 1. Agent in the miraculous conception (1) The
restoration of woman. (2) Union of God and man. 2. Anointing of the Lord Jesus for His work by the Holy Ghost.
(1) Baptism of Christ. (2) Temptation. (3) Public ministry.
(4) Sacrifice on the Cross. (5) Resurrection. The glory of the
Holy Spirit in the work of Christ. III. Conclusion. Glory of
the God-man, the new Head of the Human Race.

WHEN the tempter, in the garden of Eden,
promised to our first parents, " Ye shall
be as God," he uttered at once falsehood
and truth. Man was made to be like God : we
were intended to be " imitators of God, as
beloved children."* This purpose of the Almighty Creator was indicated in the very words
in which He announced His intention of forming
man. "God said, Let Us make man in our
image, after our likeness . . . And God created
man in His own image."†

*Ephes. iv. 1.　†Gen. i. 26, 27.

To what extent and in what sense this likeness
was lost by the Fall, has been a matter of dis-
pute; and it is a question which we need not
here attempt to decide. There is a sense in
which man still bears the image of his Maker;
and there is a sense in which fallen man must be
pronounced to be very far from being like God.
" All have sinned and fallen short of the glory of
God."* The most favorable judgment of the
human race will not contradict the doctrine of
the sinfulness of man. But God who created
man for fellowship with Himself would not
abandon His gracious purpose of restoring and
perfecting His own likeness in His creature.

This great work might be entrusted to no
creature: it must be the work of God Himself;
in the first place of the God-man, and in the
second place of God the Holy Ghost. It was said
of the Lord Jesus Christ, by the angel who
announced His birth to Joseph : "Thou shalt call
His Name Jesus; for it is He that shall save His
people from their sins;"† and the writers of the
New Testament throughout attribute the merit
of the work of redemption to the "Saviour which
is Christ the Lord."‡ But it is set forth, with
equal distinctness and emphasis, that the work

*Rom. iii. 23.
†S. Matt. i. 21.   ‡S. Luke ii. 11.

of the Holy Spirit is no less essential to the completeness of the salvation of mankind.

Most of these testimonies have reference to the application by the Holy Spirit of the work of Christ, begun on earth and carried on by His perpetual intercession in heaven. But our present business is with that earlier and preliminary work whereby the Holy Spirit prepared the God-man, the Second Adam, for His mission as Saviour of mankind. It is difficult to convey, by any single phrase, a complete idea of this work of the Blessed Spirit. The form of words which we have ventured to adopt—the Fashioner of the Second Adam—may be accepted as not altogether inadequate. Under this general notion we include the miraculous conception of Christ, when, in the words of the Creed, He "was incarnate by the Holy Ghost of the Virgin Mary," and all the gracious influences by which He was enabled to fulfil His work in the world.

i. And first let us ask what we mean by the *Second Adam ;* what He must be who shall fulfil this idea of S. Paul and of Christian theology. What are we to think of Him Who shall be to the whole human race what its first parent was, only in a higher and better sense? Of Him who shall be a new Head to mankind, a new centre and source of life, a new stem into which the branches of the human family may be so grafted that they shall become again one tree, and from which they shall draw a higher and nobler life, the life of grace and of God, a life which shall fit them for communion with the Eternal, and make them meet to enter and abide in His eternal dwelling place? What must He be from Whom such gifts and blessings should flow, and upon whom they should depend?

1. In the first place, the Second Adam must be the *Ideal Man*. The first Adam was, in the natural sphere, the perfect man in potency, if not in actual realization. "God made man upright," conforming him to His own idea of man's nature. The Second Adam must be the ideal man in a higher sense. Adam's nature was one of simple innocence, and he did not abide in his original state. He lost the gift of grace by means of which he stood. Before the new Adam can be recognized as such by the conscience of mankind, he must be more than a mere innocent, harmless child. He must be of tried and established virtue and holiness. He must be the perfect man, and must be manifested as such in a life of active service, of temptation and trial; of sorrow, suffering, and self-denial. Man, although fallen and sinful, will yet refuse to acknowledge as King of men and Crown of

humanity, One who has not realized the highest thoughts and convictions of the heart of man.

2. But there is more required in the Second Adam than mere human perfection. He is not to be a mere teacher, however elevated, nor a mere example, however perfect. If no more were needed, then a life of blamelessness and purity, an enlightened intelligence, united with a supreme gift of teaching, might suffice. But such a conception of the Second Adam is not only at variance with the whole testimony of the Catholic Church and with the fundamental idea upon which it rests: it is equally at variance with the plain language of the inspired writer and of our Blessed Lord Himself, which represents Him as the source of life to men. "In Him was life, and the life was the light of men." "God gave unto us eternal life, and this life is in His Son. He that hath the Son hath the life; he that hath not the Son of God hath not the life." "I am the way and the truth and the life." "I live; and yet no longer I, but Christ liveth in me."* It is needless to multiply quotations. To remove this idea from the New Testament would be to change its whole character and testimony; and this idea is involved in the term, the Second Adam.

*S. John i. 4; 1 S. John v. 11, 12; S. John xiv. 6; Gal. ii. 20.

Adam was not merely the typical and representative man, the pattern to which all who bore the name of man must be conformed. He was also the root of humanity, the origin of its existence and its life. So also we may say of the Second Adam that, if He is to realize the idea contained in such a phrase, He must also be the Source and Fountain of a higher life to man : the source of a divine life to the members of the human race; and this work could be accomplished only by bringing man into union with God; and this again only by first, in His own Person, taking the manhood into God.

ii.   This work of the Redeemer, this work in Christ and by Christ, was brought to effect through the agency of the Third Person in the Holy Trinity, the Blessed Spirit of God.

It is evident that such a Being, with such nature, attributes, character, could not be the product of a race like ours.   There is a clear line of division between those who regard the Gospel as of supernatural origin and those who consider it to be merely a phase or stage of human civilization.   If we reject the principle here announced, we reject the whole Christian system as it has been understood in the Church from the beginning.   We must lay entirely new foundations, and build up an edifice which the

Holy Church throughout all the world would dis-
avow as a representation of its own fundamental
and eternal character. The race of man could
not and did not produce a true King and Head
of mankind, a Second Adam. He must be, and
He was and is, of higher origin. "The second
man is of heaven."*

What was there in human nature that could
give birth even to a perfect man? Who can
bring a clean thing out of an unclean? The
experiment has been repeated often enough to
give demonstration of the result. On any com-
putation of time, several thousands of years must
have elapsed in the history of mankind before
the birth of Jesus Christ, and there had been no
departure from the universal law, "All have
sinned." The judgment of truth could only confess, "There is no man that sinneth not."†
Something, therefore, beyond nature and above
it, something higher than nature, must intervene
to produce a greater effect. The perfect man,
the ideal human being, the Second Adam, cannot be the mere child of man; He must be tho
work of God.

But if such a conclusion is forced upon us by
a consideration of the Second Adam as the ideal
man, how much more, when we think of Him as

---

*1 Cor. xv. 47.   †1 Kings viii. 46.

the Source of a new life. He who has undertaken such a work must be not merely the ideal
man, but the God man. The race of man could
be made divine only through a Head who was
Himself divine. Indeed, it is not easy to imagine
the Second Adam as the ideal man unless He
were also the God-man; and whence could He
come but from God? If nature could not produce
a perfect sample of itself, how much less could
it transcend itself? If humanity could not give
birth to a perfect man, how could one be born of
it who was God?

There is no answer to these questions but a
confession of impotency. This work must be
the work of God; and the New Testament tells
us that it was so decreed and accomplished. The
Old Testament and the New alike proclaim with
the voice of prophecy that the mighty work was
to be done through the agency of the Holy
Spirit. He was to be—and He was—the Fashioner of the Second Adam, in the first place, as the
Agent in the miraculous conception of the God-
man; and, in the second place, as the Giver of
the gifts of grace in the human life of the Lord
Jesus.

With regard to the first of these offices, we
find, as already noted, just such intimations in
Old Testament prophecy as we might expect—

predictions which could not have conveyed their full meaning to those who first heard them, and which we should ourselves hesitate to interpret, in a Christian sense, unless we had the guidance of New Testament writers.

Thus the prophecy in Isaiah vii. 14, apparently refers to a special moment in Jewish history, and, although we might feel certain that its fulfilment stretched further on, we should probably hesitate to assign to it a Messianic character, but for the interpretation of the prediction by S. Matthew (i. 22): "Now, all this is come to pass, that it might be fulfilled which was spoken by the Lord through the prophet, saying, "Behold, the virgin shall be with child, and shall bring forth a Son, and they shall call His name Immanuel; which is, being interpreted, God with us."

The same prophet speaks of the work of the Holy Spirit in preparing our Lord for His ministry on earth in a passage (xi. 2) which has already been considered, and further (lxi. 1): "The Spirit of the Lord God is upon Me: because the Lord hath anointed Me to preach good tidings unto the meek; He hath sent Me to bind up the broken-hearted, to proclaim liberty to the captives, and the opening of the prison to them that are bound"; and our Lord declared that these words were fulfilled in Him.* It is, however, in the New Testament that we find the clearest enunciation of the work of the Holy Spirit in the preparation of Christ.

1. In the first place, the Holy Spirit is declared to be the Author of the miraculous conception of Christ, a statement which demands the most attentive and serious consideration. We have been taught and we believe that Jesus Christ is the God-man. He is the Word made flesh. He is One "who, being in the form of God . . . emptied Himself, taking the form of a servant, being made in the likeness of men";† and the manner of this union of the Godhead with humanity was extraordinary and miraculous. Although the Son of man, He was not the child of a man. To the blessed Virgin Mary it was announced by the angel Gabriel: "The Holy Ghost shall come upon thee, and the power of the Most High shall overshadow thee: wherefore also that which is to be born shall be called holy, the Son of God."‡ And to the same effect it was proclaimed to S. Joseph: "Joseph, thou son of David, fear not to take unto thee Mary, thy wife: for that which is conceived in her is of the Holy Ghost."§

---

*S. Luke iv. 18.   †S. John i. 14; Phil. ii. 6-8.
‡S. Luke i. 35.   §S. Matt. i. 20.

We see, then, how deeply the Holy Spirit is concerned in the very beginning of the work of our Lord, as being the Author of the Incarnation. And this stupendous transaction is in two ways a reversal of the Fall of man. It was the restoration of woman and the assurance of her high place in the purpose of God, and it was the union of God and man.

(1.) The honour put upon the Blessed Virgin Mary was not merely the means of connecting the Second Adam with the humanity of which He was to be the Head, but also a sign that woman was restored to her rightful place in the family of man. Woman is not merely the source of the family; she is also its centre and the fountain of all those influences, good or evil, which become incorporated in the character of her offspring. God gave hope to mankind by giving a pledge of the restoration of woman.

Now, it is a recognized fact that, in all the early ages of the world, woman has been under what may be called a curse. She had been first in the transgression, and she had her own special and peculiar burden of woe to bear. She had been created as an help meet for man, yet in most parts of the world she had fallen to something hardly better than his slave. To this day the traces of that bondage are not wholly oblit-

erated even where the Gospel has proclaimed
that in Christ Jesus there is neither male nor
female. Beyond the limits of the Church it remains in almost all its ancient harshness. It
was the will of God that woman thus fallen
should be raised; and it was fit that the elevation of the sex should be brought about by the
Saviour of the world being born of a woman.

Mary was the first in the restoration as Eve
had been first in the Fall. How sweet and ele-
vating was the thought that swelled the bosom
of that Hebrew maiden, when she became aware
of the high honour which God had appointed for
her, and reflected on all the blessings that should
flow from the Incarnation to Israel and to all
the nations upon earth. " He hath looked upon
the low estate of His handmaiden: for behold,
from henceforth all generations shall call me
blessed."* The curse was lifted from the woman,
when she became the mother of the Incarnate
Son of God.

(2) But it was in another respect the reversal
of the Fall: it was the union of God and man.
By the power of the Holy Ghost the Eternal
Word took man's nature in the womb of the
blessed Virgin Mary of her substance, and by

---

*S. Luke, i. 46.

the same power the Godhead was united with
the manhood in one indissoluble personalty. In
this great transaction God and man are united,
reconciled ; and the pledge is given of a wide
and universal reconciliation. The Church in
her state of grace and of glory is already constituted in the Person of her Head.

2. But the work of the Holy Spirit in connexion with the Second Adam did not cease with
the miraculous conception. It was to be continued throughout the whole life and ministry of
the Son of God : to Him the Spirit was not given
by measure.* God anointed Jesus of Nazareth
with the Holy Ghost and with power, Who
went about doing good, and healing all that
were oppressed of the devil."†

If we are asked to explain how it was that
the Holy Spirit should have been concerned in
the sanctification of the manhood of Jesus, rather
than the Eternal Word, which was inseparably
connected with that manhood, we can but par-
tially answer the question. We might say that
the Third Person in the Holy Trinity is the
active Agent by which all the works of the Godhead are carried into effect. We might say that
it was fitting that the Head of the human race
should be brought to perfection in the same way

*S. Jno. iii. 34. †Acts x. 38.

as the members of the race. But even if we are unable to explain the mystery of the Divine action, we may yet reverently and profitably study its process and effects. And it is the distinct testimony of the Gospels that the same Holy Spirit who was the author of the Incarnation was the Framer of the whole life of the Lord Jesus.

(1) Let us begin with what we may call the point of transition from the private life of our Lord to His public and ministerial life. That point is, of course, His baptism by S. John in the river Jordan. It was an act of the most solemn character which the Baptist at first regarded as superfluous and unworthy of Him who was its subject; but which Christ Himself pronounced to be necessary, in order that He might " fulfil all righteousness."* On this occasion " the Holy Ghost descended in a bodily form, as a dove, upon Him."† It was not the first time, as we have seen, that He was anointed with the Holy Spirit, since He was miraculously conceived by the Holy Ghost, and He was " filled with the Holy Ghost even from His mother's womb."‡ But it was fitting that,

---

*S. Matt. iii. 15.   †S. Luke, iii. 22.
‡S. Luke i. 15.

at this solemn consecration of the Son of God to His public work, there should be a presence and visible manifestation of the anointing and consecrating Spirit.

When S. John the Baptist directed his disciples to that greater One who should come after him, he described Him as the Lamb of God, and in so doing he indicated not only the sacrificial aspect of His work, but also His personal character, as the meek, the gentle, the unresisting; and, if it were possible to give greater emphasis to this teaching, it would have been effected by the figure of the dove which hovered over Him in His baptism. This form proclaimed that the Spirit which should rest upon Jesus, and which was to form the predominating character of His life and ministry, was not a Spirit of mere force, or of wrath, but a Spirit of peace, and of love, and of reconciliation. The dove which went forth out of the ark when the waters were assuaging upon the face of the earth, had ever been regarded as the symbol of peace and love. "The dove is chosen as the symbol of the reconciliation of man with God, and of the universal restoration which the Holy Spirit was to produce through Jesus Christ. The first dove, with its olive branch, announces to Noah the cessation of the deluge of waters; the second, resting upon the great Victim of the world, announces the near end of the deluge of iniquities."*

It may be also, as has been suggested, that the completeness and unity of the gifts imparted to our Lord were in this manner represented. The tongues of fire might speak of the Spirit of love and of God going forth in all His manifoldness and variety, distributing to every man severally as God might will; but the one living creature, hovering over the head of the anointed Saviour seemed to speak of the fullness, completeness, and harmony of the divine life which dwelt in Him.

If devout minds have found other thoughts suggested by this appearance; if, for example, the dove has been regarded as the type of suffering innocence, and, in this respect, a symbol of the Man of Sorrows, we have nothing to urge against the suggestion; but we are probably right in making the other reference more prominent.

(2.) From the inauguration of the Lord Jesus in the river Jordan, we pass at once to the temptation in the wilderness, which must be regarded as a solemn preparation for His public ministry. And here again the presence and operation of the Holy Spirit are declared, "Jesus,

*S. Chrys. Hom. 26 on Genesis.

full of the Holy Spirit, returned from the Jordan"; and this same Spirit continued to guide Him to the conflict before Him; for "then was Jesus led up of the Spirit into the wilderness to be tempted of the devil."* The devil is the adversary, the tempter, the destroyer; and the battle between the true King of man and the usurper must be fought out to the bitter end, beginning here in fact, in symbol, and in prophecy, a battle to be often repeated with like results until the time of the last final victory and overthrow. And it is the Holy Spirit Who leads the Warrior to the conflict, Who prepares Him with the weapons of warfare and of victory. The great poet of the "Paradise Regained" makes the wilderness the scene of Satan's defeat, of the Redeemer's victory, almost the stage on which human redemption was accomplished. The temptation was, at least, the formal commencement of the conflict, and it was also the pledge of its glorious consummation.

(3.) The work which was thus begun in solitude and silence in the wilderness was carried on in public, before the eyes of the world; and it was carried on still and always by the grace and power of the Holy Ghost.

*S. Luke iv. 1; S. Matt. iv. 1.

Did the Son of Man go forth to proclaim the
good news of the Kingdom? It was by the
grace of the Holy Spirit. When He stood up for
the first time, as it would appear, in the synagogue of His own Nazareth, among the men and
women who had known Him as child, as boy, as
man, He declared: " The Spirit of the Lord is
upon Me, because He anointed Me to preach good
tidings to the poor: He hath sent Me to proclaim
release to the captives and recovering of sight to
the blind, to set at liberty them that are bruised,
to proclaim the acceptable year of the Lord."*
Are not these the gentle, loving, plaintive utterances of that Spirit Who hovered over Him at
His baptism in the form of a dove? Are they
not a fulfilment of the prophecy which had declared of Him: "Behold My Servant whom I
have chosen; My Beloved, in whom My soul is
well pleased: I will put My Spirit upon Him,
and He shall declare judgment to the Gentiles.
He shall not strive, nor cry aloud; neither shall
any one hear His voice in the streets. A bruised
reed shall He not break, and smoking flax shall
He not quench, till He send forth judgment unto
victory. And in His Name shall the Gentiles
trust."†

*S. Luke iv. 18, 19.
†Isaiah xlii. 1-3; S. Matt. xii. 18-21.

Or again, did He give evidence of His power and of the true character of His work by driving out from the bodies and souls of men the evil spirits which had taken possession of them? This, too, was effected by the power of the Holy Ghost. Surely, it was fitting that the Spirit of good should overcome and expel the spirit of evil. "To this end was the Son of God manifested," says S. John,* "that He might destroy the works of the devil"; and the confession was wrung from those who were witnesses of His works: "With authority and power He commandeth the unclean spirits, and they come out."† But, although the authority was His own, the power was that of the Spirit Who had been foretold by the prophet Isaiah, and Whom He confessed when He said, "If I, by the Spirit of God, cast out devils, then is the Kingdom of God come upon you."‡

(4.) But the work of the Divine Spirit in the ministry of Christ does not terminate with His teaching and working. The time of patient teaching and loving labour comes to an end; and the time of deeper suffering and sorrow draws nigh, the time when He must make His soul an offering for sin. And here again the

*1 S. John iii. 8.   †S. Luke iv. 36.
‡S. Matt. xii. 28.   Compare Acts x. 38.

Holy Spirit is present and working. When the
"new Isaac, the Victim of the human race,*
appears, it is the Holy Spirit Who, as the new
Abraham, leads Him to Calvary and offers Him
upon the cross." So it is expressly declared in
the Epistle to the Hebrews: He, "through the
eternal Spirit, offered Himself, without blemish,
unto God."† As it has been well said, "the
anointing of that Spirit, whose energy is the
'Fire of love,' was as a flame, amidst which He
in the freedom of filial obedience, offered Himself
up to God."‡

(5.) As might be expected, the Spirit of life
is also found presiding at the great victory and
triumph of life, for we are taught that it was
also by the instrumentality of the Holy Ghost
that the Lord Jesus was raised from the dead.
For, even if we cannot thus interpret the passage in Romans i. 4, since we must regard the
"Spirit of holiness" in that place as designating
the Divine Nature of our Lord Jesus Christ,

---

*Gaume, *Traité du Saint Esprit*, ii. 168.

†Hebrews ix. 14.

‡"In modern times many have understood by the 'Eternal
Spirit,' either our Lord's Divine nature, or His human spirit.
The use of the preposition *dia* seems scarcely consistent
with either of these views, but harmonizes with the reference
to the Holy Spirit. This reference is further supported by
the prominence given to the title *Christos* in this chapter."
Westcott, Comm. in loc.

there can be no doubt as to the application of
another passage in the same epistle : * "If the
Spirit of Him that raised up Jesus from the dead
dwelleth in you, He that raised up Christ Jesus
from the dead shall quicken also your mortal
bodies through His Spirit that dwelleth in you."

It has been truly said that the Incarnate
Word seems to ascribe to the Holy Spirit all the
glory of His success. "If He baptizes, if He
drives out evil Spirits, if He teaches the truth,
if He gives the power to forgive sins ; in other
words, if with one hand He overthrows the
Kingdom of Evil, and with the other builds up
the Kingdom of God, it is in the name and by
the power of the Holy Spirit." † Let none,
therefore, imagine that he is detracting from
the glory of the Divine Son when he is exalting
the work of the Blessed Spirit. Over and over
again we may remind ourselves of that great
testimony to the need and excellence of the
work of the Spirit. "It is expedient for you
that I go away."‡ Such is the testimony of the
Lord Jesus to the work of the Holy Spirit. Such
is the work of the Paraclete, the third Person in
the Holy Trinity, in the fashioning of the Second
Adam. He is the Author of the Incarnation,

*Romans viii. 11.   †Gaume, ii. 167.   ‡S. Jno. xvi. 7.

He is the Consecrator of the Teacher, He is the
Power of the Worker of miracles, He is the
Giver of grace and gifts to His humanity, He
presides at the Cross, and He raises Him from
the grave.

iii. We have been considering the Holy Spirit
as the Fashioner of the Second Adam. May we
not fitly for a moment turn our attention to the
glory of that New Head of the human race, the
God man?

What is the universal testimony of mankind
to this Second Adam thus fashioned by the Holy
Ghost? Men have differed in their interpretation of the doctrines of the Church; they have
differed even in their estimate of the evidences
of Christianity. But practically there has been
no difference of opinion as to the moral splen-
dour of the character of Jesus Christ. Qualities
which in ordinary men involved contradiction
in Him were united and harmonized.* Such
grace and majesty, such sweetness and power,
such simplicity and dignity, such calm and such
energy, were never before or since found united
in one person. He speaks and it is confessed
that never man spake as this Man. He com-
mands and all obey. At His word the tempest

---

*See Martensen's "Christian Ethics," Vol. i., p. 266 ff. ;
and Gaume ii. p. 170 ff.

is calmed and the demons expelled. He teaches as One who has authority. The holiness of His life is so absolute that He can challenge His enemies to convict Him of sin. He lives only to bless: He returns love for hatred, benediction for execration. He not only surpasses human experience and human expectation: He has realized the Divine Ideal of man. All that man was in the mind and purpose of His Divine Creator Jesus Christ was, "holy, guileless, undefiled, separated from sinners."*

He was the fulfilment of the eternal purpose of God and of the longing desire of man. Long had the sinful race sighed for a deliverer. Night had succeeded morning, and morning night. Week had followed week; and years and generations and centuries passed by; and still He came not. Yet the time was filling up, and its fullness came at last; and as it came, men's hearts began to swell with anticipation; and in many lands, of Jew and Gentile, they found themselves asking, Where is He that is born King of the Jews? How shall we be guided to the Desire of all nations? And why have the longings and expectations ceased, but that this Deliverer has come?

*Hebrews, vii. 26.

Yes, and to us too He has come, and we have seen His glory, the glory as of the only begotten of the Father, full of grace and truth. He is the same now as when He dwelt in the lowly Nazareth or taught in the streets of the loved Jerusalem, the same yesterday, to-day, and forever; the same in goodness and truth, the same in power and glory. And, as we behold His glory, we worship and adore, confessing, "Thou art the Son of God; Thou art King of Israel."*

It is a spectacle which may well humble us in the dust, and yet lift us up again. Well may we, as we gaze upon His perfections, cry out with Job: "Now, mine eye seeth Thee, wherefore I abhor myself, and repent in dust and ashes;"† and with Peter, "Depart from me, for I am a sinful man, O Lord."‡ But we do not remain here. There is joy and hope, as well as sorrow and self reproach, in the face of Jesus Christ. "God sent not the Son into the world to judge the world; but that the world should be saved through Him."§ If He is set for the "falling," He is also for the "rising up of many."‖ If He convinces of sin and of judgment, He also convinces of righteousness and tells of pardon and peace. "Wherefore also He

---

*S. John i. 49.   †Job xlii. 5, 6.   ‡S. Luke v. 8.
§S. John, iii. 17.   ‖S. Luke, ii. 34.

is able to save to the uttermost them that draw near unto God through Him, seeing He ever liveth to make intercession for them. *

Nor is this the whole of His work of grace. In pardoning He restores, reconciles, renews, brings into conformity with Himself, and fits for the fellowship of God. The same Holy Spirit Who was given to Him without measure, dwells forever in the Church, His mystical body, and communicates His own divine life to all its members. Even in us, in our measure, the work may be done which was done in Christ; and of His fullness we all may receive, and grace for grace. "Lord, to whom shall we go? Thou hast the words of eternal life. And we have believed and know that Thou art the Holy one of God." †

*Hebrews, vii. 25.   † S. John vi. 68, 69.

LECTURE IV.

THE CREATOR OF THE CHURCH

The dwelling of God with man the end of Creation. I. Greatness of the Day of Pentecost, By some denied. Asserted that the Church existed before, etc. Here contended.—(1) That the Holy Ghost was, for the first time, personally revealed on the Day of Pentecost; (2) That this day did institute a new stage in the Kingdom of God ; (3) That it was the Birthday of the Christian Church. II. The Creation of the Church. 1. The preparation for the Advent of the Holy Spirit.—(1) The significance of the season of Pentecost. (2) The waiting disciples. 2. The signs accompanying the revelation of the Holy Spirit.—(1) Wind (2) Tongues of fire. 3. The Creation of the Church.—A new description of the Christian Society.—(1) Family of God. (2) Body of Christ. (3) Temple of the Holy Ghost. 4. Blessings flowing from constitution of Church.—Illumination, Purification, Power.

B
UT will God in very deed dwell with men on the earth ?* What heart has not felt something of the awe inspired by such a question ? How should " the high and lofty One that inhabiteth eternity, whose name is Holy,"† condescend to make His dwelling with sinful men ? Well might we exclaim with the Psalmist: " What is man that Thou art mindful of

*2. Chron. vi. 18.　†Isaiah lvii. 15.

him : and the son of man, that Thou visitest him ?" * And yet it must be acknowledged that the asking of such a question, natural as it may appear, implies an ignorance or a forgetfulness of the very end and aim of creation ; for the universe exists as a place of abode, as a sphere of manifestation for the Most High.

To creatures of our limited capacities there will probably always remain a mystery in the work of creation. But, if the Divine Creator pronounced His successive works to be " very good," and, if they were the product of wisdom, love, and power, they must have been very good ; and if he placed at the summit of His creation a being who was made in His own likeness, then we are sure that the created world was intended to be a dwelling place for the Creator, and that man, the crown of creation, was made for communion with God.

It is by his being made of a divine nature that man is qualified for such high fellowship ; and it is in proportion to the realization in his own being of the Character of God that he will be able to have "fellowship with the Father " and sympathy with the spirit of the Kingdom of God. To bring mankind into this condition may be

*Ps. viii. 4.

said to be the whole aim of Divine Revelation. To discipline and mould the members of the human family into conformity with the mind of God, so that they should find true and abiding satisfaction only in the knowledge and fellowship of God—this is the work of Providence and of Grace, of Divine Revelation in all ages, of the Law and the Prophets, of the Incarnate Son, and of the Holy Ghost, the Comforter.

If it is by being made like unto God that man is enabled to enter into fellowship with Him it is equally through the revelation of God that the character of man is assimilated to that of his Maker. It is when " with unveiled face," we reflect " as a mirror the glory of the Lord," that we are transformed into the same image."* And this work of Divine manifestation is carried forward throughout the whole course of human history, " from glory to glory," shining more and more unto the perfect day.

It is in the Incarnate Son that we see most fully displayed the glory of God. No man knoweth " the Father, save the Son, and he to whomsoever the Son willeth to reveal Him."† He alone could say, " He that hath seen Me hath seen the Father." ‡   But even His manifestation

*2. Cor. iii. 18.   †S. Matt. xi. 27.   ‡S. John xiv. 9.

did not complete the work which was given Him to do. God and man were united in Him, and in His Person, that of the Second Adam raised and glorified, the race of man was lifted up into the presence and glory of God. But the work needed to be completed on earth by other instrumentalities, and by the two great Representatives left by Him as His witnesses upon earth—the Church, which is His mystical Body, and the Holy Spirit who, after having created the Church, dwells in it as a living Temple.

i. Two things were necessary in order to the Creation, the existence of the Church of God: firstly, the offering of Christ as a Sacrifice and His assumption in glory, and secondly, the gift of the Holy Spirit. It is, therefore, the Creation of the Church by the Holy Spirit, on the Day of Pentecost, that we are now to consider.

These points have generally been considered settled by students of the New Testament and Christian theologians. As, however, they have been called in question in a recent "History of Christianity in the Apostolic Age"*— a work showing learning and ability—it may be well to consider the statements there made on the subject. The author, the Rev. Dr. McGiffert, makes the following statements: "There is no

* By A. C. McGiffert. Ph.D., D.D. (T. & T. Clark, 1897.)

indication in our sources that Jesus thought of
the coming of the Spirit as instituting a new
stage in the Kingdom of God, or as constituting
the establishment of the Kingdom in any sense."*
And again, † "The Day of Pentecost, immediately succeeding the death and resurrection of
Jesus, has always been regarded as of epochal
significance for the history of the Christian
Church . . . That it was an important day in
the history of the Church there can be no doubt,
but its importance is not that which is ordinarily
ascribed to it. It was not the birthday of the
Christian Church, as it is so commonly called,
for the Christian Church was in existence before
Pentecost; nor was it the day upon which began
the dispensation of the Holy Spirit, for His promised coming preceded, or, at least, was closely
connected with, Jesus' own return to His disciples
after His resurrection."

Passing over some apparent contradictions and
ambiguities in these statements, we venture to
affirm, in opposition to their principal conten-
tions, (1) that the Holy Ghost was for the first
time personally revealed on the day of Pentecost,
(2) that this Day did institute a new stage in the
Kingdom of God, and (3) that it was the birthday
of the Christian Church. The first of these state-

* P. 33, Note.   † P. 48.

ments has already been sufficiently dealt with.*
But there is one point on which something may
seem necessary to be said, namely that the
" promised coming of the Holy Ghost" took
place before.

(1) Such an assertion we hold to be quite inconsistent with the words of our Lord at His
ascension, as repeated twice by S. Luke. In his
Gospel† we read the words of Christ: " Behold I
send forth the promise of My Father upon you :
but tarry ye in the city, until ye be clothed with
power from on high ;" and in the Acts of the
Apostles,‡ we read as follows : He " commanded
them that they should not depart from Jerusalem,
but wait for the promise of the Father, which, saith
He, ye have heard of Me. For John truly baptized with water, but ye shall be baptized with
the Holy Ghost, not many days hence." It
seems totally unnecessary to comment at length
upon these passages. The promise of the Father,
the Gift of the Holy Ghost, was to come to them
at Jerusalem after the ascension, and it did
come, according to the same writer, on the Day
of Pentecost.

Although, however, the meaning of these passages seems clear enough, it may be necessary

---

* In Lec. ii.   †S. Luke xxiv, 49.   ‡Acts i. 4, 5.

to refer to another incident which might seem at variance with them. We refer to what appears to have been the first manifestation of our Lord to the Apostles after His resurrection, when "He breathed on them, and saith unto them, Receive ye the Holy Ghost." *

In regard to this incident it is obvious to remark that it is not a fulfilment of the predictions relating to the coming of the Holy Spirit, and the solemn promise of Christ, that His disciples should receive power when the Holy Ghost was come upon them, was given many days after this occurred. How then do we explain these words of our Lord, and the act which accompanied them? It must be regarded not merely as an anticipation of the Gift of Pentecost, but as a special endowment of the Apostles qualifying them for their work.

"As the Father hath sent Me," He said, "even so send I you. And when He had said this, He breathed on them, and said unto them, Receive ye the Holy Ghost; whosesoever sins ye forgive, they are forgiven unto them, whosesoever sins ye retain, they are retained." It was, in fact, the organization of the Christian Church by anticipation. We need not stop to ask whether

* S. John, xx. 22.

the words were spoken to the apostles officially,
or to the disciples as representing the Church at
large, because the decision of that question has
no direct bearing upon our present inquiry, nor
would it necessarily affect our judgment in regard to the Christian ministry. Here, at any
rate, we find our Lord conferring authority to
admit into and exclude from the privileges of
the New Covenant, bestowing by anticipation
upon the Church which He was about to organ-
ize what is called the "power of the keys."

We can understand, without difficulty, the
reason for such a provision. The Church was
not to be a Republic with popular government:
it was not to derive its authority and power from
below, but from above, even from Jesus Christ,
its Head; and, although the fullness of His gifts
was to dwell in the whole body, the teaching and
ruling members were to be in direct and immediate connexion with Himself, deriving their
authority from Him. When the new life should
be breathed into the dry bones by the presence
and breath of the life-giving Spirit, and bone
should join to bone, and flesh should cover and
clothe them all, every one should be in his own
order, and all should be symmetry and harmony.
And this work, no less than the greater and
more comprehensive work, should be accom-

plished by the Third Person in the Holy Trinity. And, therefore, our Lord breathed upon them and said, "Receive ye the Holy Ghost." It was only when "He ascended on high" that He "gave gifts unto men "* in the full sense of the words; but even on earth He had power, and He exercised the power to set in order the house in which He was Son and Master; and He began that work in which He gave, in due order, "some to be apostles; and some prophets; and some evangelists; and some pastors and teachers; for the perfecting of the saints, unto the work of ministering, unto the building up of the Body of Christ." †

(2.) In regard to the second statement, we maintain that the Day of Pentecost did institute a new stage in the Kingdom of God, whether we regard that phrase as having its usual significance of the Reign or Dominion of God, or whether it stands for the establishment of a Divine society on earth. In the first place, there can be no question as to the Coming of the Kingdom being connected with the Advent of Christ   It is, of course, true enough also that we may speak of the coming of the Kingdom in

* Psalm lxviii. 18; Ephes. iv. 8.
† Eph. iv. 11, 12.

the person of its King. Yet not merely St. John
the Baptist, but our Lord also, after the beginning of His ministry, declared that the Kingdom
of God was at hand, and He taught His disciples
to pray : " Thy kingdom come." In its primary
sense that prayer was answered when He sat
down upon His mediatorial throne, when all
power was given unto Him in heaven and in
earth, when being " by the right hand of God
exalted, and having received of the Father the
promise of the Holy Ghost, He poured forth " *
that gift upon His disciples accompanied by
visible and audible tokens.

From that time there is no intimation of the
coming of the Kingdom of Grace and even the
Kingdom of Glory is not so indicated.

Our Lord, when preparing the Apostles for the
gift of the Holy Spirit, was "speaking the things
concerning the Kingdom of God,"† and in the
preaching of the apostles and evangelists, after
the day of Pentecost, it is assumed that the
Kingdom is come and may be entered. Thus
Philip is represented as " preaching the good
tidings concerning the Kingdom of God,"‡ and
when his countrymen came to St. Paul at Rome,
to hear his message, " he expounded, testifying

* Acts, ii. 33. † Acts i. 3. ‡ Acts viii. 12.

the Kingdom of God, and persuading them concerning Jesus.*

(3) Still more energetically must we contend
against Dr. McGiffert's statement that the Day
of Pentecost is not the birthday of the Church,
because, as he says, "the Christian Church was
in existence before Pentecost." We maintain,
on the contrary, that the Christian Church was
brought into existence on the Day of Pentecost,
by the creative power of the Holy Spirit.
This point requires some careful consideration on account of the variety of meanings in
which the word "church" is employed by
theological writers.

Thus we hear of the Old Testament Church
and the Church of the New Testament; and if we
take the word (*ecclesia*) in its ordinary meaning
of an assembly, or in its more literal, and perhaps more scriptural meaning, of an assembly
solemnly called out, then the application may be
justified. Abraham was called out by God, and
formed the type and the beginning of that dispensation which prepared for the Gospel, and
found its fulfilment in the Church of Christ.
The children of Israel were a chosen and peculiar people, a holy nation to God, and might
properly enough be described as the family that

* Acts xxviii. 23.

was "called out" of the general mass of mankind
by the guidance and grace of God. In this meaning S. Stephen might speak of them as "the
Church in the wilderness."

But it is obvious that this is not the special
New Testament use of the term. The word is
used once in the Gospels with reference to the
particular Jewish congregation with which a
man might be connected;* but it regularly represents the Christian society of baptized
believers. This society had no organized existence before the Day of Pentecost. Up to that
time the followers of Jesus were called disciples;
but by the power of the Holy Spirit these separate individuals were made to be an organized
whole, a living body, in which every member
had its own place and function, contributing to
the completeness and harmony of the whole—
all the members depending upon the Head, all
being members one of another. All this was
done by the power of the Holy Spirit on the Day
of Pentecost, and this is, therefore, the Birthday
of the Church.

Let us, for a moment, remember how much
had been done in preparation for this great day.
The Second Adam had been supernaturally and
miraculously conceived in the womb of the

* S. Matt. xviii. 17.

Blessed Virgin. He was Himself the Kingdom of
God and the Church in representation, in germ,
and in power. Much was done afterwards.
The temple of God, although in one sense complete at its first foundation, was to be raised
laboriously and painfully throughout many ages;
the living stones being fashioned and fitted upon
the foundation of apostles and prophets by the
Master Builder who first gave the building form
and life. But it was on the Day of Pentecost
that the disciples of Christ became the Church
of the living God, that the distinct members
were organized and knit together into one living
unity, soon to become the mystical Body of the
Lord. This, therefore, is the principal point to
be considered when we speak of the Holy Spirit
as the Creator of the Church.

ii. Respecting the great event of Pentecost we
have two sources of information, first, the history contained in the Acts of the Apostles; and
secondly, the meaning of the event which we
learn chiefly from the epistles. It is principally
from the history that we must derive our knowledge of the facts, and from the epistles of S.
Paul that we learn to understand the meaning
of what actually took place. In undertaking
this study it is of interest to consider (1.) the preparation for the Advent of the Holy Spirit; (2.)

the work of the Spirit in the Creation of the Church; and (3.) the blessings accompanying and resulting from the constitution of the Church.

1. It was evidently the intention of our Lord to impress the disciples with a deep sense of the necessity, the greatness, and the efficacy of the Gift of Pentecost. This is brought home to us both in the language employed in his valedictory address respecting the coming of the Paraclete, and in the instructions which he gave his hear-ers on Ascension Day, as to their waiting and preparing for the gift and presence of the Holy Ghost. These directions, twice put on record by S. Luke, need not here be repeated. The disciples were commanded to wait for the promise of the Father. They were to receive power when the Holy Ghost was come upon them.

We see how reverently the Apostles complied with the requirement of their Lord. How the ten days between Ascension Day and Pentecost were spent we are not told; but we may judge from the manner in which they were begun and ended. In united prayer and supplication they chose, under Divine guidance, an apostle into the room of the traitor, " and when the Day of Pentecost was now come, they were all together in one place." *

* Acts ii. 1.

(1) We can hardly be mistaken in assuming that there was significance in the season which was chosen for this manifestation. Just as the resurrection of Christ took place at the time of the Feast of First Fruits, signifying that He is "the first fruits of them that are asleep";* so the descent of the Holy Ghost took place at the Feast of Harvest, signifying that the presence and fruits of the Holy Spirit would be to the world that great harvest for which the Son of God had laboured, and of which He, in His resurrection, had been the beginning.

If it be true, according to the Jewish tradition, that the Law was given through Moses at the same season, we may perceive in this coincidence a suggestion of deep interest. We are, in fact, reminded that the Law of the Spirit has taken the place of the Law of the letter, that the "Law of the Spirit of life in Christ Jesus" has made us "free from the Law of sin and of death";† that the law which was expressed in precepts and written upon "tables of stone," gave way to the higher Law of one supreme principle—the principle of Love, written in tables that are hearts of flesh.

There may also be significance in the day of the week. The first day of the week was, in

*₁ Cor. xv. 20.   † 2 Cor. iii. 3.

many respects, memorable. It was the day of
the creation of light, and of the resurrection of
Christ from the dead, so that it might fitly be
chosen as the day of the new creation of the
Church by the Divine Spirit, who, at the first
creation, brooded upon the face of the waters,
and was also the Agent in the resurrection of
our Lord from the grave.

(2.) Turning from the time to the circumstances of the event, we are struck by the character of the Christian assembly who are waiting
and looking for the fulfilment of the Master's
promise. The number present is not mentioned
—they may have been the same as those who
took part in the election of Matthias; nor are
we told what the place was, whether the same
"upper chamber" or not; but simply that "they
were all *together* in one place." The later reading, *with one accord*, doubtless expresses accu-
rately the unity of sentiment prevailing among
them. The notice thus afforded is of interest
and importance.

The disciples of the Lord were in a state of in-
tense expectation and hope, waiting for the
fulfilment of His promise, for the supreme blessing which He had announced. The Spirit of
love and unity and union was about to descend;
and the first fruits of that Spirit they had already

received. But if their condition was in part a result of the work of the Holy Ghost, it was no less a fitting preparation for His Advent; and it is well for us to study the attitude of those to whom this stupendous favour was granted by God. They were fulfilling the behest of their Divine Master, who had promised that special blessings should be granted to them, if two or three of them should agree. They were all together in one place, bent upon one object, and, as we may judge from other passages, engaged in earnest entreaty or in patient waiting for the promised blessing. So much for the preparation and circumstances of the disciples on this great day. Let us now consider the event for which they had been waiting.

2. " Suddenly there came from heaven a sound, as of the rushing of a mighty wind, and it filled all the house where they were sitting." Every word here is full of meaning. The event came suddenly: there was, at the appointed moment, a distinct Divine interposition. It was, in a certain sense, an answer to the prayers of the disciples; but it was also the fulfilment of the Divine promise. It was the work of God, and this thought is made more emphatic by the addition of the words, "from heaven." The gift came down from God out of heaven; nay,

rather, it was God and heaven coming down to dwell with man on the earth. Even here we have a hint of the great change which is now passing upon the Family of God, and an intimation of that blessed and glorious union of heaven and earth which is to be realized in the Church.

(1). And what was the sign by which the heavenly presence was declared? It was " as of the rushing of a mighty wind," one of the most powerful agencies in nature, and one which leaves behind it the most remarkable traces of its influence. The wind is a mighty power; it tears up and casts down the mightiest trees of the forest; it raises the waters of the sea into heaps and mountains, and opens up its depths to the eyes of men. The Spirit of whom it is a symbol is a spirit of power, a mighty agent, Who comes with a new and unknown strength to change the face of humanity and to stir it to its depths.

The wind is also a purifying agent. A breeze, springing up in the time of sickness or plague, has sometimes proved the saving of thousands of lives. A strong blast of wind has dispersed the brooding vapors of pestilence and infection, which were hanging over the habitations of men, and thus has restored life and health to those who were trembling on the very brink of

the grave. But a greater and more effectual
Purifier is He who is symbolized by the wind,
for He can banish the infection of evil, and
drive away the pestilence of sin from the hearts
and wills of men.

The wind, again, is the symbol of life. In all
languages it is the synonym of spirit. We
speak of the "breath of life." When God made
man "He breathed into his nostrils the breath
of life, and man became a living soul."* We
speak of the God "in whose hand our breath
is;"† and the very words which tell of a spirit
of man, of the Holy Ghost in the Godhead, signify in their primary meaning a breath or a gust
of wind. Well, then, might the coming of the
Spirit of God, the Life-giver, who was to bestow
upon man, through the Church, a new principle
of life, be heralded and announced by "a sound
as of the rushing of a mighty wind."

(2) This was the sign which smote the ear.
The eye was also taught by the appearance of
"tongues parting asunder like as of fire"; but
the Power that was in the midst of them was
greater and more irresistible than the tempest,
was more burning and devouring than the fire,
for it was the Presence and Power of God Himself; nay, it was God Himself come to dwell

* Gen. ii. 7.   † Dan. v. 23.

with man upon the earth, fulfilling the promise of the Father and the work of the Son. When the Word was made flesh, then God dwelt in personal union with the Man Christ Jesus, but now He comes to dwell in mystical union with the whole Church, which He constitutes as an habitation in the Spirit.

3. This was the work of Pentecost, the creation of the Church by the power of the Holy Ghost. To the change then effected in the significance of the company of believers, we have already referred. Hitherto they had been known as "disciples," and although they do not lose that name, they gain another. They now become the Church. At the election of Matthias we read: "Peter stood up in the midst of the disciples."* The name is an honorable one and is oft repeated.† Yet after this time we find the regular designation of the body of believers to be The Church.‡

It is difficult to realize in thought, and it is still more difficult to convey by words, a true idea of the enormous change, the miracle of grace which had been wrought by the Advent of the Paraclete, and which is expressed by the

---

* Earlier manuscripts have "brethren."
† Acts vi. 1, 2, 7 ; ix. 1, 19, etc.
‡ Acts v. 11 ; viii. 1, 3 ; ix, 31, etc.

phrase, the Creation of the Church. It would
not be accurate to compare it to the change
wrought in the dry bones by the breath of God
in the vision of Ezekiel; for these were disciples and believers, and had a real spiritual life
which they lived by the faith of the Son of God.
Nor would it convey the exact truth to say that
these isolated living branches were now, by the
grace of the Holy Spirit, united to Him who is
the Fountain of Life, for in a true sense they
were already the branches of the True Vine.

We may yet employ some such figures as these
to denote our sense of the change effected in the
disciples by the event of Pentecost. Before this
time they believed in Jesus, they were taught
and influenced by Him, they obeyed Him ; nay,
more, they had received great and gracious gifts
from Him through the Holy Spirit. But now,
by the personal descent and manifestation of the
Holy Spirit, they were in a deeper and more inward manner made to participate in His life;
they were drawn into a closer union with Christ
and with one another, so as to have a common
participation in His risen life, and to be made
one body and one spirit with Him. Is it a
mystery ? Man is a mystery to man and to himself. Truly we may well confess that there is
mystery when we think and speak of the things

of the Spirit of God, and of the work which He dwells on earth to perform for man on behalf of our risen Lord who is now within the veil.

(1.) " This mystery is great ; " says S. Paul ;* "but I speak in regard of Christ and of the Church." The depths of this mystery we shall never sound ; yet we may learn much from the language in which inspired writers labour to set forth the truth concerning the Church. Thus, to begin with a conception which comes home to the experience of all, the Church is the *Family of God*. " Beloved," says S. John,† " now are we children of God." To this privilege we have attained in our present condition ; and to this privilege we have been brought by the Gospel through union with the Great Elder Brother. The filial Spirit was comparatively unknown under the law. The heir, as long as he was a child, differed but little from the bond-servant. "But when the fulness of the time came, God sent forth His Son born of a woman, born under the law, that He might redeem them which were under the law, that we might receive the adoption of sons. And because ye are sons, God sent forth the Spirit of adoption into our hearts, crying, Abba, Father."‡ The presence of the Holy Ghost imparts the

*Ephes. iv. 32.   † 1. S. John iii. 2.   ‡ Gal. iv. 1-6.

spirit of adoption, of sonship; and thus the disciples of Christ become the Family of God.

(2.) No less significant, and even more striking,
is another figure under which the Church is represented, namely, the *Body of Christ.* It is a
conception which is not only plainly set forth in
the New Testament, but which forms the basis
of much teaching and earnest exhortation. Thus
it is said of our Lord Himself, " In Him dwelleth
all the fulness of the Godhead bodily ";* and the
Church is declared to be " His Body, the fulness
of Him that filleth all in all." † It is an astonish-
ing revelation of Divine truth which is made to
us by means of this symbolism, if we may so
describe it. It bids us think of this work of the
Holy Ghost as so knitting men to Christ, and
binding them into spiritual union with Him,
that He and His members become one, we might
almost say identical. He is the Head, and He is
also the Body, comprehending the whole organism; yet they are also the Body, the members
of that mystical constitution, the hands by which
He acts in the world, the lips by which He speaks
to the children of men, the feet by which He still
goes forth on errands of mercy. We are thus
told of a union subsisting between the members
of Christ so close, so intimate, that they are not

* Col. ii. 9.   †Eph. i, 23.

only, in common, members of Him, but also
"members one of another,"* having "one spirit
one Lord, one faith, . . . one God and Father,"†
one life. We are told that the life of the mystical Body, that Life which is the cause of its
organization and existence, and the power by
which it subsists, is God the Holy Ghost, proceeding from the Father and the Son, entering
into each member with His own Divine life,
making it a living part of the Body, and dwelling in the Body as an organism, through which
He manifests His power and glory.

(3.) And then there is another type under
which the nature of the Church is set forth, that
of a Temple, a living habitation for God by the
Holy Ghost. It is not only a beautiful image,
but a thought which might be inferred from the
conception of the Body. For the Body of Christ
is the Temple of God. "Destroy," He said,
"this Temple, and in three days I will raise it
up. . . . But," says S. John, "He spake of the
Temple of His Body."‡ It is a beautiful image
in its application to the Church, a structure
"built upon the foundation of the apostles and
prophets, Christ Jesus Himself being the chief
corner stone; in whom each several building
fitly framed together, groweth into a holy temple

* Rom. xii. 5. † Ephes. iv. 4-6. ‡S. John ii. 19, 21.

in the Lord; in whom ye also are builded together for a habitation of God in the Spirit."*

Such was the work which the Holy Ghost came to accomplish on the Day of Pentecost and which He actually brought to effect, and which by His abiding presence on earth He has made permanent and will continue to preserve until the Lord Jesus shall come again. It is a work not unworthy of Him who, at the beginning, brought order out of chaos, and who by His Divine power was the Fashioner of the Second Adam; for He is now the Author of a nobler creation than the first, and it is by His power and working that the Incarnation is so extended as to draw Humanity into true and living union with God through Him who is its Head.

(4.) This brings us to consider briefly some of the blessings flowing from the Constitution of the Church, especially as indicated by the visible phenomena of Pentecost.

The most remarkable of these was the appearance of "tongues parting asunder, like as of fire," resting upon each one of those present. A more significant symbol could hardly be imagined. Speech is, in truth, the highest gift of God to man; it is the expression of that rea-

*Ephes. ii. 20, 22. Compare 2. Corinth. vi. 16: "We are a temple of the Living God; even as God said, I will dwell in them."

son which elevates him above the beasts that
perish. The mere animal does not speak, because he does not possess that power of thought
which utters itself in articulate language. So
closely is the Word connected with the Reason
that the same word stands for both in Greek,
and it has even been debated whether the *Logos*
in S. John should be translated The Reason or
The Word.

Naturally, therefore, the tongue is spoken of
as a great power in human life. "If a man
offend not in word," says S. James, "the same is
a perfect man."* If we could become acquainted
with a man's whole conversation, in his lighter
and in his graver moments, and mark the subjects to which his thoughts and speech naturally
turned, we should know his character. "By
thy words," said our Lord, "thou shalt be justified, and by thy words thou shalt be condemned."† And S. James reminds us that it
is not merely an effect in human life and an
evidence of its internal character, but also a
powerful cause of its movements. It is like the
helm of a ship which, although it be "very
small," yet turns the ship about, "whither the
impulse of the steersman willeth."† It is the
Eternal Word who reveals the invisible God,

---

* S. James iii. 2.   † S. Matt. xii. 37.   † S. James iii. 4.

and it is by the word of truth that men are
sanctified and saved. The Holy Spirit came to
the disciples on the Day of Pentecost, to complete
and perfect the instruction which Jesus had
given. The tongue resting on each Christian
head told of truth to be revealed to the intelligence, and spoke of a new power introduced into
human life which should affect man's innermost
thoughts and come out in all his words, which
should rule that member which ruled the whole
man.

But, let us note, these tongues were tongues
"like as of fire." There is an agency no less
significant and potent than the wind. By one
or other of these agents nearly all rapid motion
is produced. By wind and by fire our ships
plough the ocean. By the same agents the grain
which waves in our fields is turned into the
staff of life. By fire we are swiftly conveyed
from land to land; by a spark our thoughts are
flashed, almost instantaneously, to the uttermost
ends of the earth. Fire is the great destroyer,
cleanser, separator. All that is most precious
is purified by fire. Hence the most remarkable
Divine manifestations were commonly accompanied by the appearance of fire. So it was when
Jehovah appeared to Moses at the bush. Such
was the Shekinah in the wilderness. Such was

the manifestation at the transfiguration of Jesus;
and so it was at Pentecost. "Our God is a consuming fire,"* and God is here; for it is God
Himself who now comes to dwell with men, to
remove the coldness of selfishness and death, and
to kindle men to life and love, to drive away
the darkness of nature and of sin, and to shed
abroad the light of grace and holiness; to purify
men from evil, to raise them up from all that is
low, and earthly, and base. It was the new Law
of the Church of God, given by fire, as the
ancient Law had been given, but not amid
thunder and lightning, but with the gentle light
of love, and with a sound as of the rushing of a
mighty wind, which spoke of the presence of an
irresistible power.

The meaning and application of this gift will
come to be considered at greater length in succeeding lectures, but we might here note one
significant feature in this supernatural manifestation. The tongue of fire rested upon each one
of the disciples present. There was not one ex-
empted from the gift and the blessing. Now,
this gift has not been withdrawn from the Church.
The Paraclete, the Blessed Spirit of God, was
given that He might abide with us for ever; and
He now dwells in the mystical Body of Christ

*Heb. xii. 29.

that He may impart life to all its members and infuse the Spirit of love into their hearts and lives. They that are Christ's are still and ever under the guidance of this Spirit; for "if any man hath not the Spirit of Christ, he is none of His."*

* Rom. viii. 9.

LECTURE V.

THE TEACHER OF THE CHURCH

Greatness of the Teacher. Revelation progressive. Culminates in Christ and the Holy Ghost. I. Holy Spirit the Teacher before Christ. Predictive element in Prophecy. Connected with supernatural character of Revelation. II. Holy Spirit carrying on teaching of Christ. Christ still teaching but through the Spirit. By various means. 1. The apostles. Special commission, guidance, illumination. 2. All Christians. Illumination promised, given, sufficient for guidance. 3. The Church taught as witnessing and ruling. Authority and infallibility. Development.

IT would be impossible to exaggerate the greatness and dignity of the office and work of the teacher. He responds to man's primary and most urgent need—the need of knowledge, light, truth, guidance. We now wonder, and the wonder will grow, that there should ever have been a time when education was thought to be unnecessary or even dangerous. It would seem to be self-evident and undeniable that knowledge is better than ignorance, and truth more useful than error.

If a man were to set himself gravely to prove that work may be done as well and as successfully in the dark as in the light of day, we should regard him as of imperfect intellect; but the mind needs light no less than the body, and it cannot produce light from itself: that must come from without. It must have a teacher.

The teacher not only responds to man's first needs: he also appeals to that which is noblest in man, to that supreme reason which makes man the crown of creation and reproduces in finite form the infinite nature of God. And He who was the Maker of men has Himself condescended to be their teacher. And such a teacher was needed by men. Much indeed could be done, much was done, by the exercise of the faculties with which man was endowed. Patient observation and thought conquered the secrets of nature. The collective experience of mankind, handed down from age to age, supplemented and directed the efforts of individual enquirers. Men of higher intelligence, of greater power of concentration than others, rendered assistance to those who were less richly endowed. We should be doing no real honor to God or to Divine Revelation by underrating the great achievements of the human mind in the course of its protracted history, for these, too, were of God; yet, on the other hand, it would be unreasonable to deny that the knowledge possessed by the human race, especially in relation to the highest objects, lacked certainty and completeness. There were many questions which men could not help asking which they were unable to answer. Even when answers were given, they often raised questions instead of giving assurance and producing conviction.

All knowledge is useful, but there is one kind of knowledge which is supreme and all comprehending—the knowledge of God, without which there can be no true knowledge of man or of the world; and it is the great aim of Divine Revelation to communicate this knowledge to mankind, as they are able to receive it. By word and by act Almighty God, throughout all ages, has spoken to eye and to ear, if by any means He might find an entrance for the truth into mind and heart. At one chosen moment in the history of the world the great predestined Teacher appeared, that Teacher for whom all others had been making preparation, and to whom every voice of truth that had spoken or should speak, was a witness. He was Himself the truth and the revelation of the truth. In Him was gathered up the sum of truth, human and Divine.

Yet the work and teaching of Christ did not complete the religious education of the world.

Even although in Him "are hid all the treasures
of wisdom and knowledge,"* yet preparations
needed to be made for the communication of
knowledge, and methods had to be employed
adapted to the character and condition of those
who were to be taught. Such has ever been the
way of the Most High with the children of men;
and Jesus Christ plainly told the disciples that
there was much to be made known to them,
even after his earthly ministry was ended. "I
have yet many things to say unto you, but ye
cannot bear them now."† Nor was this all.
Another agent was to be employed in carrying
on the work of instruction. "When He, the
Spirit of Truth has come, He shall guide you
into all the truth." And, earlier in the same
discourse He had said: "The Comforter, even
the Holy Ghost, whom the Father will send in
My name, He shall teach you all things, and
bring to your remembrance all that I said unto
you."‡ Here, then, it is plainly declared that
the teaching work of Christ was to be carried on
and completed by the Holy Spirit.

i. Before, however, considering more particularly the work of the Paraclete as Teacher of
the Church, it is necessary to say something on
His preparatory work in the world, in the He-

*Coloss. ii. 3.   †S. John xvi. 12, 13.   ‡S. John xiv. 26.

brew economy, and in the ministry of Christ.
It is not merely the teaching of the Scriptures, it
is a truth involved in the relations of the Godhead and in the nature of man that all spiritual
illumination comes from the Holy Spirit, and
this equally whether it is what we should call
the ordinary or the extraordinary enlightenment
of the mind. We do not say supernatural, because in truth all divine operation on the Spirit
of man is supernatural : It is not of nature, or of
man, it is of God, it is of grace. But, on the
other hand, there is afforded to certain chosen
organs of divine revelation a kind of inspiration
beyond and above that which is communicated
in the ordinary course of spiritual illumination.

This double thought is obvious or latent in the
whole structure of the sacred writings. On the
one hand, it is asserted or assumed that all
spiritual enlightenment is from the Spirit of God.
Indeed we might go further than this, and say
that all knowledge and wisdom and skill is attributed to the same origin. "There is a spirit
in man," says Elihu, "and the Spirit [or Breath]
of the Almighty giveth them understanding ;"*
and the Lord, speaking to Moses † of the man
whom He had appointed to fashion the Taber-

* Job xxxii. 8.
† Exod. xxxi. 1-4.

nacle, said "I have filled him with the Spirit of God, in wisdom and in understanding."

On the other hand, it is distinctly implied that there is entrusted to certain specially privileged men the gift of special revelation and inspiration, which is the work of the Holy Spirit. Various efforts have been made to explain these gifts. Thus revelation has been described as the communication of truth, and inspiration as the elevation of the mind in order to the perception and comprehension of truth. Or, again, it has been said that Christ is Himself the whole sum of revelation, and it is the work of the Divine Spirit to throw light upon that revelation, in His Natures, Person, Work, relations to God and Man.

Even if we cannot search into the depths of the things of God, we may yet, in this way, come to understand better the significance of the Blessed Spirit's work of grace in the human heart. But at least there can be no doubt of the teaching of Scripture on the extraordinary inspiration accorded to those who were specially commissioned to make known to men the Counsels of God. Thus, we read that inspired men prophesied, "searching what time or what manner of time the Spirit of Christ which was in them did point unto, when it testified before hand the sufferings of Christ, and the glories that should follow them." * So again, " We have the word of prophecy . . . whereunto ye do well that ye take heed . . . knowing this first, that no prophecy is of private interpretation. For no prophecy ever came by the will of man; but men spake from God, being moved by the Holy Ghost."† So in another passage, ‡ however we may translate it, there is implied that certain writings have been produced under the influence of special inspiration: "Every scripture inspired of God is also profitable for teaching, for reproof, for correction, for instruction which is in righteousness." Thus, then, we see that the spiritual education of mankind was carried on not only by oral communications such as were made to Moses in the giving of the Law and in the instructions for the guiding of the people, but also by the inspiration of the Holy Spirit, who, although He was not yet personally revealed, was yet truly present in the world, illuminating and sanctifying the people of God, and also revealing by specially selected agents the mind and purpose of God towards Israel and mankind.

An attempt has been made, not only in our own days, but in earlier times as well, to eliminate the predictive element from the prophet-

---

* 1 S. Peter i. 10-12.   † 2 S. Peter i. 19-21.   ‡ 2 Tim. iii. 16.

ical utterances and writings, and restrict them
to the enunciation and elucidations of spiritual
truth. There would be no difficulty, we suppose, in conceding the superior importance of
the disclosing of the essential mind and will of
God in comparison with the announcement of
events in the future, however important. But
it is impossible to deny the existence of the predictive element—that the prophets did actually
profess to foretell events which were to take
place in the future—without doing violence to
any theory of divine authority which might be
ascribed to the books of the Bible, or the
Apostles, or even the Son of God Himself.

The prophets did profess to foretell future
events. They were understood to do so. Our
Blessed Lord attributed this character to their
work, and Himself predicted events in the future
history of His Church. Not only is it continually taken for granted and asserted that prophets were commissioned by God to make known
what was to happen in the future, but the
validity of his commission was to be tested by
the fulfilment of His prophecy or otherwise.
Thus we are told : * " When a prophet speaketh
in the name of the Lord, if the thing follow not,
nor come to pass, that is the thing which the

* Deut. xviii. 22.

Lord hath not spoken ; the prophet hath spoken it presumptuously."

One should suppose that the testimony of our Lord would be conclusive on this subject. Of the Old Testament Scriptures in general He declares : * " Search (or, ye search—it matters not which rendering we adopt) the Scriptures, because ye think that in them ye have eternal life ; and these are they which bear witness of me." So of special predictions He declares that they are fulfilled ; and in regard to the future, He told His disciples of the things which were coming upon the world, upon Jerusalem, upon the Church, and based solemn warnings upon these announcements.

It would be impossible, in this place, to discuss this subject at length ; but it may be said, and it is not too much to say, that the question of prediction in prophecy is closely, perhaps inseparably, connected with the supernatural character of the revelation of Christ. If coming events ever may be expected to cast their shadows before, surely this might well be, when the coming events were the Incarnation of the Eternal Word of God in the Man, Christ Jesus, and the descent of the Holy Ghost, the third Person in the Blessed Trinity, to create on earth a dwell-

* S. John v. 39.

ing place for Himself. We may deny these stupendous events, and decide on our own responsibility that there is no supernatural character in the Bible or in the Central Character of the Bible, the Lord Jesus Christ; but we can hardly accept the Catholic faith in Christ and in the Church, and, at the same time, deny the probability of such things being announced beforehand by God to men. We must hold, on grounds of Scripture and reason alike, that the predictions of the prophets were the outcome of the inspiration of the Holy Ghost.

As we have already seen, the Holy Spirit was an Agent in the teaching of the Lord Jesus when He was here on earth. The Spirit of the Lord was upon Him when He stood up for the first time in the Synagogue of Nazareth; and the same agency was recognized throughout His ministry. It is, however, more especially with the teaching of the Holy Spirit after the Ascension of Christ and the Creation of the Church on the Day of Pentecost that we have here to do.

ii. Our Lord's words on this subject are most clear and explicit. Much that He had to communicate His disciples were not prepared to receive. But they would enter into a new sphere of experience when He was taken away from them in bodily presence, and the Holy

Spirit should come in His place as Teacher.
Yet, even then, the teaching of the Spirit would
be but the development and completion of the
teaching of Jesus. This thought is presented to
us in various forms. Thus, in one part of the
valedictory address, our Lord says: "The
Comforter, even the Holy Spirit, whom the
Father will send in My name, He shall teach you
all things and bring to your remembrance all
that I said unto you." * And again, "He shall
not speak of Himself . . . He shall glorify
Me; for He shall take of mine and declare it
unto you." †

If Jesus Christ is the Truth and the sum of all
revelation, in Whom are all the treasures of
wisdom and knowledge, then we can understand
the relation of the work of the Holy Spirit to
that which He had accomplished during His
ministry upon earth. But we can also understand that there was much of the work of Christ
which could be made intelligible to men only
after He had passed within the veil. While He
was still here He could tell men, in general
terms, that the Son of Man had come to give His
life a ransom for many; but it was not possible
that He should convey to His disciples all the
significance of His mediatorial work, all the

---

* S. John xiv. 26.   † S. John xvi. 13, 14.

truth concerning the graces and gifts of the Holy Spirit, as it was afterwards made known by the Apostles under the guidance of that Spirit.

There was, indeed, much in the teaching of our Blessed Lord which could be conveyed only in a partial, a concrete, and even a paradoxical form, until the Divine Spirit should come and reveal the principle which underlay those precepts which we are apt to find inapplicable to our present circumstances. If, for example, we should attempt to reduce to practice the precepts and counsels of the Sermon on the Mount, we should undoubtedly decide that, as a code of morals or of laws, these precepts could not be practically applied to our modern life. If, however, they are interpreted in the light of the Spirit of love and sacrifice, the beauty of their meaning will be seen at once.

Well, then, let us inquire into the manner in which the Divine Spirit carries on this work of teaching and illumination. And here, without penetrating far into the regions of controversy, we soon become aware of a very startling diversity of views.* For example, we encounter one school of writers who think that the promise of the Comforter was to the apostles alone, and that the whole substance of the teaching pro-

*On this subject consult Hare's " Mission of the Comforter."

mised to be communicated through the Holy Spirit is contained in the New Testament. On the other hand, there are those who maintain that the apostles had no more than the ordinary guidance of the Holy Spirit vouchsafed to Christians in general, and that their writings are simply the utterance of Christian thought and Christian experience. Then, among those who hold that there is such a thing as the development of Christian doctrine after the time of the apostles, there are considerable diversities of opinion in regard to the manner in which the truth of such development should be tested.

Without endeavoring to follow out the various lines of thought which open themselves before us, we may note the principal ways in which, as we believe, the Divine Spirit carries on the teaching work of the Lord Jesus in the Church. In the first place, there were special gifts of teaching and special guidance accorded to the apostles of Christ. In the second place, there were the ordinary gifts of grace and answers to prayer granted to all Christians in general; and, in the third place, there was special guidance bestowed upon the Church for the decision of controversy and the promulgation of the truth.

1. We may not be able to define these various gifts and endowments in such a manner as to

produce perfect satisfaction in the mind of the
student of Divine truth; but the distinctions
here suggested may serve for general practical
guidance. To the apostles we may reasonably
assert that their Master granted such guidance by His Spirit as to secure them from error
in the teaching of the Church. To individual
Christians, although it would be presumptuous
to claim inerrancy for them, yet we might say
that such guidance would be afforded, where
sincerely and earnestly sought, as would be
practically sufficient. With regard to the Church,
whilst infallibility could not be claimed, there
might yet be such an assurance of Divine guidance as should furnish a foundation for the
exercise of authority.

Let us remember that, in this teaching,
whether of the individual Christian, or of the
inspired Apostle, or of the Church at large, the
source is at once the Eternal Word and the
Divine Spirit. Just as the teaching of our Lord
during His earthly ministry was not independent
of the anointing of the Spirit, so the teaching of
the Paraclete after the Day of Pentecost was not
separate from or independent of the teaching of
the Lord Jesus. A good illustration of the joint
work of the second and third Persons in the
blessed Trinity is furnished in the Epistles to the

Seven Churches of Asia, in which each Epistle begins with a name or title of our Lord as the Supreme Speaker who addresses the Christian Communities as their King, while each one equally attributes the message to the Holy Spirit: "He that hath ears to hear, let him hear what the Spirit saith to the churches."

The thought that our Lord, after His ascension, is still the Teacher of the Church, is made prominent both in the Epistles and in the Acts of the Apostles. At the very beginning of the Acts it is declared that the teaching and the working of the Church, which are recorded in that book, were not only the effect of the ministry of the Paraclete, but a continuation of the teaching and working of our Lord Jesus Christ. "The former treatise I made," says the writer, "concerning all that Jesus *began* both to do and to teach, *until* the day in which He was received up"—hereby implying that He was now, in this second treatise, continuing a narrative of all that Jesus went on to do and to teach after His ascension.

We have said that the teaching of the Paraclete was carried on through the Apostles. This is the first and most obvious fulfilment of the promise made by our Lord. These men had a special commission from Christ. He had com-

manded them to preach His Gospel throughout
the whole world. He had promised to be with
them. One subsequently added to their number
had a special call. Everywhere the new apostle,
S. Paul, proclaimed that his office of apostle was
not of man, but of God and through Jesus Christ.
The signs of an apostle accompanied his teaching,
and his words brought conviction to the minds
of his hearers. He commended himself " to
every man's conscience in the sight of God." *

Controversies have arisen with respect to the
inspiration of the apostles; but, if we put aside
prejudice and theory, the matter presents no
great difficulty. S. Paul writes as he spoke, as
one who had instruction and guidance from
Christ. Sometimes, he tells us, he has no special
instruction from his Master; at other times, he
says, he is giving the commandment of the Lord.
Practically, there is no difficulty in ascertaining
his meaning. The Church has followed a true
instinct, and has taken the only course rationally
open to her in basing all her teaching upon the
utterances of inspired writers. Whether there
are any other sources of Divine knowledge or
not, whether we can add to the teaching of
apostles and evangelists or not, it is impossible
that we should contradict or change the teach-

* 2 Cor. iv. 2.

ing of those who were guided by the Holy Spirit
and the Word of Christ. This must be, to us,
the foundation of all revealed truth, and, as
such, it has always been held in honour by the
Church.

2. Whilst, however, we maintain the supreme
authority of Holy Scripture, we can by no means
agree with those who would restrict the action
of the Holy Spirit to the writings of the apostles.
The promise of spiritual illumination and guidance is given to all the followers of Christ, to all
the members of His Church. Although the great
valedictory discourse was primarily addressed to
the apostles, the promises therein contained
applied to the whole Church, and when the Holy
Ghost came down from heaven, the tongues of
flame, which were the signs of His presence,
rested upon the heads of each and all of those
present.

It is not merely the promise of our Lord; it is
involved in the very nature of our relations to
Him, that every member of His Church should
have a personal guidance from the Holy Spirit.
"If ye being evil," said our Lord, "know how
to give good gifts unto your children, how much
more shall your heavenly Father give the Holy
Spirit to them that ask Him."*

*S. Luke xi. 13.

It may be true that men have misunderstood the nature and extent of this guiding. When, for example, men venture to elevate their own personal opinions to the dignity of dogmas because they have prayed for light, and believe that they have obtained a certain answer, we must regard such pretensions as savouring not of faith, but of presumption. This would be indeed to make not one infallible teacher in the Church, but multitudes, not to constitute one authoritative seat of judgment, but to set throne against throne and oracle against oracle. Such a theory is not founded on Scripture or Reason; it is a product of mere fanaticism.

Yet we may not for that reason deny that God does give, by His blessed Spirit, such guidance to individual Christians as meets their personal needs and affords them all necessary guidance. Inerrancy, indeed, is not promised, but such practical certainty as suffices for their position and requirements. "If any of you lacketh wisdom,* says S. James, "let him ask of God, who giveth liberally and upbraideth not; and it shall be given him. But let him ask in faith."*

The conditions of such endowment are clear and reasonable. There must be an honest and

*S. James i. 5, 6.

good heart on the part of the seeker; there must be a use of such means as the Providence of God has placed within his reach, the diligent study of the Holy Scriptures; the devout use of the means of grace, and there must be the asking with which the Hearer of prayer refuses to dispense. "Ye have not because ye ask not. Ye ask and receive not, because ye ask amiss."* Practically there is here no difficulty as to the Divine promise and its fulfilment in our own experience. Almighty God has not promised to answer curious or useless questions. He has not promised to aid us in the settlement of controversies which are the outcome of human conceit and impatience. But we may be well assured that, wherever men are humbly desirous of knowing the mind and will of God respecting their own relations and duties, they will not fail to obtain such guidance as will give them practical certainty in the conduct of their life; the wisdom which they lack will be supplied to them according to their need, in full and sufficient measure.

3. There is, however, another aspect of the teaching of the Holy Spirit which demands attention and consideration, the guidance afforded to the Church as a witness for the truth in the

*S. James iv. 2, 3.

world. There can be no doubt that the apostles
individually received from the Lord and by the
inspiration of the Holy Ghost a full revelation of
the Gospel message and of the demands which
were made upon those who professed their faith
in Jesus Christ as the Saviour of mankind. We
remember how earnestly S. Paul maintained his
independence as an apostle, his authority derived
from the Lord Jesus, and the truth of the Gospel
which he proclaimed.

All this is quite plain. But there were questions on which the apostles themselves did not
profess to have at once received complete information and guidance, and there were questions which they had to consider and decide in
common. For example, when the question
arose as to the admission of the Gentiles into
the Church, S. Peter for a season was in doubt
until he was assured by a vision from heaven
that nothing that God had cleansed was to be
regarded as common or unclean.* And when
other questions arose, as to the rules to be im-
posed upon Gentile Christians, and some Judaiz-
ing brethren made circumcision "after the
manner of Moses,"† a condition of salvation, it
was felt that this was not a question to be
settled by individual opinion, and therefore

*Acts xi. 9.   †Acts xv. 1, 2.

"they determined that Paul and Barnabas, and certain other of them, should go up to Jerusalem, unto the Apostles and Elders, about this question."

Some such resolution was inevitable and obligatory. The disciples of Christ were no longer a mere assembly of believers associated by common interests and common principles; they were an organized society, a Church. As such, it was of necessity that they should have rules and laws by which the members of the society should be bound, and that the society should promulgate those rules by authority as a condition of membership. This would be necessary in any organized body.

But this was a Divine Society, founded by and upon Christ, to which He had given the promise, " Lo, I am with you alway, even unto the end of the world ";* and in which His Spirit, another Paraclete, Advocate, Comforter, should abide for ever. Accordingly, when these grave questions arose, affecting the deepest spiritual interests of the infant community, the leaders in the Church came together and took counsel, on the one hand giving testimony as to the guidance already received from the Lord, and on the other hand, casting themselves upon the promised aid of the Holy Spirit.

* S. Matt. xxviii. 20.

The Council of the Apostles at Jerusalem, commonly and properly considered to be the first Council of the Christian Church, may, indeed, be rightly regarded as a model for all such assemblies. The leaders of the Church came together with a deep sense of the gravity of the occasion. They heard the testimonies of Peter and Barnabas and Paul; the President of the Assembly, James, Bishop of Jerusalem, summed up the consultations and gave utterance to the decision of the assembly; and finally there came forth from the Council letters to the Church, setting forth the decrees as not merely coming from the apostles and elders at Jerusalem, but as being sanctioned by the Divine Spirit: "It seemed good to the Holy Ghost and to us." *

It was quite natural that there should afterwards come to be associated with utterances of this kind the idea of infallibility; and to the ordinary mind it may often be difficult to separate the ideas of authority and infallibility. Yet, a moment's reflection may satisfy us that the one does not involve the other. The possession of authority is inseparable from every rightly-constituted society. We recognize authority in the family and in the state. Unless we would return to chaos, we must have authority also in the

* Acts xv. 28.

Church. But this does not carry with it the idea of inerrancy or infallibility in other spheres; and there is no reason to think it should do so in the Church. The later notion, that this infallibility should be lodged in one particular see, was unheard of in earlier times.

If it is said that we are thus endangering any authoritative teaching on the part of the Church, we have two answers. In the first place, we have the sacred writings of the disciples of Christ and the Creeds promulgated by authority and received by the whole Church; and those who break loose from these restraints are properly excluded from the communion of that Body which is a witness to the truth. In the second place, the demand for absolute certainty and infallibility is one which has no sanction from Reason, Experience, or Scripture. Moral certainty, or high moral probability, is the utmost that man can expect in this world. Those who ask for more than this are asking for something which they will not obtain in any other department of life.

A question closely connected with this subject may properly receive some brief consideration —the question of the development of Christian doctrine. Now, whatever subordinate difference may exist on the question, it is at least certain

that, in some sense, we all believe in a doctrine
of development, that is to say, that the doctrines
of the Christian religion may properly be expressed in forms beyond those which are found
in the New Testament. As an example of such
development we need only point to the Nicene
Creed. We believe that the whole doctrine of
this creed is involved in the teaching of the
Apostles; yet it contains phrases which are nowhere found in their writings.

The principle of a true development would
seem to be a very simple one, that no doctrine
should be regarded as part of the Christian
faith which had not its germ in the teachings of
the Apostles ; and that no portion of the original
deposit should be set aside on the plea of adapt-
ing the teaching to the changed circumstances
of later times. By this principle we condemn
on the one hand that so-called development
which eliminates the substance of truth and of
the doctrine which it professes to develop ; and
on the other, that equally spurious system which
introduces doctrines absolutely new, of which
no germ or trace is found in Holy Scripture or
in the teaching of apostolic men.

The test of the truth of a doctrine, in the judgment of early Christianity, was its acceptance
by the Church at large; and perhaps there is

not, and never will be, a safer test. A council,
however carefully and regularly organized, has
never been regarded as having absolute authority until it received the assent of the Church.
The Second Council of Ephesus seems to have
lacked nothing in regard to the regularity of its
constitution, yet it was stamped as the Robber-
Synod and discredited by the Church. The first
council of Constantinople was but a comparatively
small local synod, yet its addition to the Nicene
Creed has become part of the Catholic faith,
because the Church has received it.

And so it will be to the end, although we may
no longer give to the principle formal recogni-
tion. Opinions are promulgated, theories are
suggested; and they may either help or hinder
the student of Divine truth; but they are
weighed in the balances of experience, they are
tried by reason, by conscience, by the Divine
word; and they live on, stamped with the
superscription of truth, or they are cast into the
waste pit of spurious coin. The world judges in
time, and its judgment is final. No act of man
can kill the truth or keep falsehood alive.

Before passing away from the subject, there
is one thought which we should impress upon
ourselves with special earnestness. We have
spoken of the different ways in which the Holy

Spirit conveys religious truth to the Church; and it was pointed out that the personal reception of the truth must largely depend upon the spirit and manner in which it is sought. There is no principle of greater importance to the seeker after Divine Truth. She does not disclose her secrets to every comer; on the contrary, she guards them jealously and keeps them from the view of all who refuse to comply with her demands. And what is it she demands of those who desire to be initiated in her mysteries? She requires humility and reverence, she asks for earnestness and self-sacrifice, and she demands an honest intention to apply and profit by her instructions.

If we could receive truth without any desire to appropriate it and live by it, no blessing could thus come to us. We must love it and desire it, and seek for it as for hidden treasure; and above all, we must come with lowly, child-like hearts. "1 thank, Thee, O Father, Lord of heaven and earth," said our Blessed Lord, "that Thou hast hid these things from the wise and prudent, and hast revealed them unto babes." Only to these and such as these will Divine Wisdom reveal herself. "Except ye be converted and become as little children," ye cannot enter into her secrets.

LECTURE VI.

——

THE LIFE-GIVER.

——

EVERY good thing is included in the idea of
life. Fulness of life is fulness of blessing.
Death is synonymous with separation,
discord, dissolution. Life brings with it harmony, unity, power, development. These two

states are accordingly contrasted in Scripture as representing the good and the evil of man. To our first parents the reward of obedience was continued access to the Tree of Life; the punishment of disobedience was Death. "Of the Tree of the Knowledge of Good and Evil, thou shalt not eat of it: for in the day that thou eatest thereof thou shalt surely die." * On the other hand, when our Blessed Lord spoke of the blessings which He came to bestow, He declared: " I came that they may have life, and may have it abundantly." † In abundance of life is comprehended every blessing for man's whole nature. Well, then, might the Hebrew Law-giver propose this alternative to his people in the name of the Lord: " I have set before thee life and death, the blessing and the curse." ‡

It is easy, therefore, to understand how this unique good should be specially represented as coming from God and resulting from the action of the Spirit of God. If all things are of Him, if every good gift is from above, then of Him Who is " the living God," § Who has " life in Himself," ‖ it might well be declared with peculiar emphasis: " He Himself giveth to all life and breath and all things."¶

* Gen. ii. 17.   † S. John x. 10.   ‡ Deut. xxx. 19.
§ Deut. v. 26 ; Psalm xlii. 2 ; Dan. vi. 26 ; Heb. x. 31.
‖ S. John v. 26.   ¶ Acts xvii. 25.

But here we are met by the question : What
is Life ? and this is a question to which neither
the theologian nor the man of science has ever
given a satisfactory answer. Many attempts
have been made to furnish a definition of Life ;
but the utmost that has been attained has been
a more or less complete description of the idea
represented by the word. We believe it to be
an active principle, for we speak of the vital
principle and vital force. We know that it is
connected with organized forms, that it has certain powers of maintaining, extending, and
propagating itself ; and that, in order to do so,
it assimilates to itself that which is without itself. It has been defined or described as the
state of an animal or plant in which the organs
perform their functions ; and again as "correspondence with environment," so " that the degree
of life varies as the degree of correspondence,"
and "perfect correspondence would be perfect
life." *

Life, as known to us, is conditioned by such
correspondence, by a connection with the world
or with the source from which it draws its support, and by a normal state of the organization
with which it is connected. Where these are
found there is life ; where they are wanting or

* H. Spencer, " Data of Biology," S. 35.

interrupted, there is death : where they are imperfect, there is disease.

And here arises another question : Whence
comes life, and how is it produced in this world ?
And to this question a variety of answers has
been given. As for ourselves, although we will
not entirely ignore the answers given by others,
we can give but one answer : The source of life
is God. The giver of life is the Holy Spirit of
God, that personal Divine energy who proceedeth from the Father and the Son. This is
equally true of natural life and spiritual life.
Such is the teaching of the sacred Scriptures, of
Reason, and it is not contradicted by any true
Science, but rather supplies that completion to
scientific inquiry which Science confesses itself
incompetent to discover.

i. NATURAL LIFE.—The Source of Natural
Life is the Holy Spirit of God. We make this
statement in clear and sharp opposition to those
who hold a materialistic theory of the world,
and profess to be able to account for all existence without assuming the existence of a creative mind.

Now, there are parts of the theory of evolution with which we have no quarrel. The truth
or falsehood of these parts is a matter of perfect
indifference to the theologian. Indeed, the doc-

trine of evolution in general is perfectly reasonable; is sustained by scientific investigation,
and derives support from Scripture. It is when
it is attempted to show that life emerges from
inanimate existence by a spontaneous generation; that the organic can spring from the
inorganic, without the introduction of any
foreign principle, that we enter our protest in
the name of Reason and of God

Let us glance for a moment at the process of
evolution as it is generally understood. There
was a period, it is said, when only inorganic
matter was known on this globe of ours. We
need not go beyond this period, nor question the
assumption referred to. There came a moment,
however, when along with this inorganic matter
the organic began to appear; when within dead
masses there appeared a cell, or whatever was
the unit of organism, with indefinite powers of
extension and development.

Whence came this primordial living form?
Some time ago the answer was hazarded: By
spontaneous generation.* It cannot be said that
this theory maintained its place for any length
of time. Indeed, it could hardly seem even a
probable hypothesis, either to the philosopher or

* Strauss, " Der Alte und der Neue Glaube"; Büchner,
"Kraft und Stoff"; Bastian, " Beginning of Life."

to the man of science. The fundamental conviction that nothing can be expected from any
cause which had not a potential existence in
that cause, will seem to forbid such a theory
imperatively and decisively. Still, it was
thought by some that experiment bore out the
truth of the doctrine of spontaneous generation.
Dr. Bastian declared: " Both observation and
experiment unmistakably testify to the fact,
that living matter is constantly being formed *de
novo*, in obedience to the same laws and tendencies which determined all the more simple
chemical combinations."

The result of inquiries into the trustworthi-
ness of these statements should induce a greater
caution in promulgating unproved theories. We
have said that such a doctrine was *a priori* im-
probable; and the investigations of Professor
Tyndall and others satisfied them that the so-
called inorganic substances operated upon by
Bastian actually contained organic matter, since,
in experimenting upon absolutely germless matter, they found not a trace of life appearing.
As a consequence, the theory of spontaneous
generation has been abandoned by men of
science. The doctrine of Biogenesis, that life
can come only from life is now generally
recognized, or, as Professor Huxley has said, is

*"victorious along the whole line at the present day"; and Professor Tyndall has declared:† "I affirm that no shred of trustworthy experimental testimony exists to prove that life in our day has ever appeared independently of antecedent life."

We hope we may not be considered unscientific if we say that such a conclusion is exactly what we should have expected, when we remember that the principle of causation is a postulate which lies at the foundation of all induction, and that life from death would seem of the nature of an effect without a cause. If, however, the philosopher and the man of science are forced to these conclusions, they are made clearer and fuller in meaning by the theologian and the student of the Scriptures. If there be a God, the Cause and Beginner of all things, there must be in Him, and must go forth from Him, that fulness of life which is progressively manifested in the structure and development of the world: and the Bible tells us that by the Word of the Lord were the heavens made, and all the hosts of them by the breath of his mouth."‡

It is not necessary for us to assume any special theory as to the history of Creation given at the

---

* " Critiques and Addresses." p. 239.
† " Nineteenth Century," 1878, p.507.
‡ Psalm xxxiii. 6.

beginning of the Book of Genesis. The general
truths set forth in that passage are found
throughout the whole of the sacred volume, and
they are confirmed by the investigations of
science and by the light of reason. Holy Scripture, no less than Science, takes us back to
chaos, and speaks of a time when "the earth
was waste and void, and darkness was upon the
face of the deep." * But there was a principle
of life hovering over this unorganized mass ; for
"the Spirit of God moved upon the face of the
waters," and His Divine energy went forth in
accordance with the utterance of the Word of
God, and all was changed. Life began to manifest itself in the waters and on the dry land, and
as day succeeded day, or epoch succeeded epoch,
a question with which we need not here concern
ourselves, fresh and higher forms of life appeared and succeeded each other in the history
of our planet.

Thus we see that the Scriptures teach us that
not only in the beginning when order, and life,
and movement were made to appear for the
first time, but throughout all the subsequent
processes and developments, the Holy Spirit was
the Giver of Life, and Reason testifies to the
same truth ; nor can Science contradict this

* Gen. i. 2.

doctrine, or offer us a theory which can supplant it.

There are some points of great interest in the Biblical account of Creation, upon which we might profitably dwell for a moment, The production of the lower forms of life is described in the most general way. But when from the origination of the lower creation we are led to the formation of man, there is a striking change. Of the earlier stages it is said : "Let there be light, and there was light." "Let the earth bring forth," "and it was so." But when man is to be introduced there is a change of style. There is, as it were, a solemn pause ; and then there is a deliberate Divine act which is described in all its circumstances. We should remark, it is still by the action of the same Divine Spirit that the event is accomplished ; but the process is set forth in detail. "The Lord God formed man of the dust of the ground, and breathed into his nostrils the breath of life, and man became a living soul."

This is no accidental statement. Without referring particularly to passages such as the one just quoted, concerning the joint action of the Word and the Breath of God, or that other which says, "Thou sendest forth Thy Spirit and they

* Gen. ii. 7.

are created," or others to the same effect,* every
higher endowment of man is, in different ways,
attributed to the Divine Spirit. In a previous
lecture † reference has been made to the case of
Bezaleel, in illustration of a special gift of knowledge and skill, and S. James tells us that "every
good gift and every perfect boon is from above,
coming down from the Father of Lights," ‡ from
Whom all things proceed, and Who giveth life
and breath and all things by the power of the
Holy Spirit.

It will not be supposed that we are thus iden-
tifying the gifts of Nature with the gifts of
Grace, or placing human intelligence on a level
with the supernatural illumination of the Spirit;
yet we must never forget that the duty of consecrating all that we are and have to God rests
upon the fact that we ourselves, body, soul, and
spirit—all that we are and all that we have—
are of God, that the Holy Ghost is the Giver of
life in the whole extent of the meaning of these
words.

ii. LIFE IN CHRIST.—When we proceed to
consider the higher life of man, spiritual life, the
life of grace, the life of God in the soul of man,

* Psalm xxxiii. 6; civ. 30. Compare Heb. xi. 3; 2 S.
Pet. iii. 5.

† The Teacher of the Church.   ‡ S. James i. 17.

the Holy Spirit is here found to be, in the emphatic sense, the Life-Giver. But here, again, we must lay stress upon the truth that the work of the Spirit is dependent upon the work of Christ.

In thus connecting the work of Christ with the Kingdom of Grace as its very foundation, we are not denying the doctrine that the Logos, the Eternal Word, is the Archetype of Creation as well as the Worker of Redemption. We are simply limiting our view by the special nature of our subject ; and it is obvious to readers of the New Testament that the work of grace carried on by the Holy Spirit is based upon, and has continued reference to, the work of redemption by Jesus Christ. We must, indeed, continually bear in mind that, as the Second Adam was fashioned and anointed for his work on earth by the Holy Spirit, so the work of the Divine Paraclete in the Church and in the world is a continuation and application of the work of Christ. When, therefore, we are to think of the Holy Spirit as the Giver of Spiritual life, we must not for a moment forget that the life of God for man is treasured up in Christ. "The witness is this, that God gave unto us eternal life, and this life is in His Son." *

* 1 S. John v. 11.

1. The Scriptures teach that man, in his natural state, without Christ, is dead. Of this there can be no doubt whatever. We may understand the language employed in different senses; but it must, at least, have a very solemn meaning, and this we shall feel the more as we consider the use of the words life and death throughout the whole record of Divine Revelation. It will not be necessary to examine critically the texts which bear upon this subject. They are so numerous that some specimens will suffice, and the general meaning will be beyond controversy.

Begin with the utterances of our Blessed Lord: "I came that they may have life." "I came to call sinners." So S. Paul: "You did He quicken when ye were dead through your trespasses and sins";* and again: "You, being dead through your trespasses and the uncircumcision of your flesh—you, I say, did He quicken together with Him."† And S. John declares: "He that hath the Son hath the Life; he that hath not the Son of God hath not the life."‡ And such language is justifiable. If we will think what the true life of man is, that it is the life of God, the life of love, then we shall see that no other word could better describe man's condition of aliena-

---

* Ephes. ii. 1. † Coloss. ii. 13. ‡ 1. S. John v. 12.

tion and selfishness than this word death. If life is correspondence with environment, and man's complete environment is God, then man without Christ was dead, for he did not correspond with his environment.

2. It was to bring life to those who were dead that Christ Jesus came into the world. The antithesis is presented in Scripture under different forms. Sometimes it is condemnation and salvation. Sometimes it is perdition and life. Sometimes it is death and life. "God so loved the world that He gave His only begotten Son, that whosoever believeth on Him should not perish, but have eternal life." * This word Life is ever prominent. "I am the way, and the truth, and the life." † "Our Saviour Christ Jesus," says S. Paul, "abolished death, and brought life and incorruption to light through the Gospel"; ‡ and again: "The free gift of God is eternal life in Christ Jesus our Lord."§

That the whole work of our salvation is properly attributed to each one of the three Persons of the Holy Trinity is a thought with which we are all familiar. Each is, in a somewhat different sense, the author of our life, natural

* S. John iii. 16. † S. John xiv. 6.
‡ 2 Tim. i. 10. § Rom. vi. 23.

and spiritual; and it is fitting that the gift of spiritual life should be specially attributed to Him who provided this unspeakable blessing by His Incarnation; by His life of poverty, sorrow and suffering; by His sacrificial death, and by His glorious resurrection and ascension. This is true and is for ever to be had in grateful and loving remembrance. But it is no less true that the Holy Ghost is the Giver of Life.

Illustrations are somewhat hazardous when we are dealing with subjects so deep and mysterious; and especially when they involve a fresh application of imagery employed in a somewhat different manner in earlier times. Yet we will venture, simply by way of illustration, to say that we may conceive of the Father as the Fountain of Life, the Son as the Channel, and the Holy Ghost as the Stream. The Father is the Fountain of all, and even of the very Godhead; for He alone of the Three is " neither created, nor begotten, nor proceeding." So He is, of necessity, the ultimate Source and Fountain of all life. But the Son is the Channel. It is through Him alone, according to the unvarying teaching of the New Testament, that the gift of life can flow into the souls of men. "I am the way and the truth and the life: no man cometh unto the Father but by Me." The Holy Ghost, the Giver of life, could not be manifested until Jesus was glorified. But we must equally maintain that He, the Holy Spirit, is the Stream, the very water of life. When Jesus spoke of the rivers of living water that should flow from those who came to Him and drank, S. John tells us, " This spake He of the Spirit which they that believed on Him were to receive "; * and we can hardly be mistaken when we see a representation of the Holy Ghost, the Giver and Water of Life, proceeding from the Father and the Son in that apocalyptic vision, in which the Seer of Patmos is shown " a river of water of life, bright as crystal, proceeding out of the throne of God and of the Lamb." †

3. And now let us examine a little more nearly the account which the New Testament gives of our new spiritual life in Christ. It is the life of grace, as distinguished from the life of nature—of grace in the subjective, not in the objective sense, of grace in us, not of grace in God, although the one is the result of the other, is dependent upon it, and is akin to it. We must, of course, here remember that, in speaking of life, we have the difficulties already remarked, and even greater, for the life of nature is more tangible than the life of grace. Yet the very

* S. John vii. 39. † Rev. xxii. 1

use of the word shows that there is an analogy,
a resemblance between the two.

If the natural life is a force, then the life of
grace is also a force. As the soul is the life of
the body, so we may say that grace is the life of
the soul. As the living body lives by virtue of
its correspondence with nature, so the living
soul lives by virtue of its correspondence with
God. It is the presence of God in the heart. It
is "the life of God in the soul of man." It is a
mighty and wonderful change which makes
man "a new creature," which makes the human
divine. It is God giving Himself to man, so that
he becomes a partaker of the Divine nature,*
and like to God. The soul of the Christian becomes the dwelling place, the temple, the throne
of God.

This change in the soul of man is the work of
the Spirit of God. The life of grace is, as we
have seen, a life of union with Christ in God.
The eternal life which God has given unto us is
in His Son. Just as we are members of His
mystical Body, so are we partakers of His life.
He has declared that He is the Vine and His people
are the branches. And the union between Christ
and His members is the work of the Holy Ghost,
"for in one spirit were we all baptized into one

* 2 S. Peter i. 4.

Body." * This, then, is plain, that the spiritual
life of man is in Christ, and that it comes to men
as they are united to Him. In Him, the second
Adam, God and man are united in indissoluble,
personal union. From Him, as Head, all grace
descends upon His members, and we have now
to consider how that union is effected.

iii. LIFE TO THE WORLD.—In considering
how the Life of God, treasured up for man in
Christ, takes effect in the lives of men, we might
begin with the conception of the Church and its
members, or we might ask how the Gospel message is conveyed to the world, which is lying in
sin and death. Either way might be justified,
and we shall hardly be making a mistake if we
ask first how the Gospel carries life to the world.
In doing so we shall do well to take the words
of our Lord for our guide. He tells us that the
Holy Ghost, "when He comes will convict the
world in respect of sin, and of righteousness,
and of judgment." † This is the preliminary
and fundamental work of the Spirit in bringing
the world, which is lying in sin and death, to the
righteousness and life of Christ—to produce the
three-fold conviction of sin, of righteousness,
and of judgment.

* 1 Cor. xii. 13.
† S. John xvi. 8. This subject is treated with great fulness in Archdeacon Hare's "Mission of the Comforter."

The necessity of such conviction will appear, if we remember that the world is not naturally aware of its need, and must be convinced of that need before it can even think of a supply. If we think of Christ as the Giver of Life, this will not concern mankind unless they are made aware that they are in a state of death. If we think of Him as a Saviour, how will this affect us, if we do not know or believe that we are sinners?

1. Our Lord, therefore, begins with the conviction of sin and the work of the Holy Spirit in producing this conviction. Conscience, by itself, had not been able to do it; for conscience had been perverted by the evil with which it was connected. The Law of God could not do do it. It is true, indeed, that "through the law cometh the knowledge of sin"; * and the law is a potent instrument in the hands of the Spirit. Yet by itself it could convict only of particular transgressions; it could not reveal to men their deep and radical sinfulness. It could forbid the act, but it did not usually touch the motive. Even the teaching of Christ Himself did not completely produce conviction, although His teaching and His example demonstrated the depth, the spirituality, and the universality of

* Rom. iii. 20.

the Law. More was still needed, and for this
the Holy Ghost was given. Nor was His coming
in vain. Compare the effect of the teaching of
Christ with that of Peter's on the Day of Pentecost. Multitudes hitherto unaffected "were
pricked in their hearts."

And our Lord tells us of the manner in which
this conviction is produced. "He shall convict
the world in respect of sin because they believe
not on Me." It was not merely of sins but of sin,
not merely of wrong acts but of the wrongness
of heart and mind from which these acts proceeded, that the world had need to be convicted.
The Holy Spirit was to show them that this
wrongness consisted in unbelief; and this had in
fact, been the root of human sin from the beginning. So it was with our first parents in Paradise. So it was with the Israelites in the wilderness. So it was during the ministry of Jesus;
and this sin of unbelief came to a head when the
Son of God was revealed to the world, and rejected by those to whom He came. Well might He
say of those who turned away from His light in
their love of darkness, "Now have they both
seen and hated both Me and My Father." * It was
this fact which S. Peter employed on the Day of
Pentecost, and it was this which the Holy Ghost

* S. John xv. 24

applied to the consciences of the assembled multitudes so as to produce in them the consciousness of sin. "They were pricked in their heart, and said unto Peter and the rest of the Apostles, Brethren, what shall we do?"*

2. But the conviction of sin must be accompanied by another, the conviction of righteousness. Consider what we mean by sin. Sin is a principle which is more negative than positive. If it takes an attitude of positive antagonism to God and to goodness, it is yet, in its own nature, a standing apart from good. It is therefore impossible for us to understand sin, unless we understand the righteousness from which it is a departure. Is there such a thing as right, imposing an obligation upon the conscience and will? If not, then there is no such thing as wrong, as sin. We know how Almighty God has answered this question. By the most awful sanctions He has declared that His will is for righteousness, and that opposition to His righteous will involves sin and guilt.

Hence the necessity of the conviction of righteousness; and this conviction is wrought by means of Christ's return to the Father. And this in a twofold sense. The Holy Spirit convinces of sin as unbelief. But there could be no

* Acts ii. 37.

sin in unbelief unless Christ were righteous; and His personal righteousness is proved by His ascension into heaven. This ascension, again, was proved by the descent of the Holy Ghost Who thus brought home the conviction of the righteousness of Christ. But it was not only His personal righteousness, but also His justifying righteousness that was thus commended. He "was delivered up for our trespasses and was raised for our justification." * By His descent, as a consequence of the elevation of Christ, and by His inward working in the hearts of men brought to the knowledge of this truth, the Holy Spirit brought home the conviction of the personal and justifying righteousness of Christ.

3. And then this work is made complete by the conviction of judgment. It is not enough to discern the spiritual opposition and antagonism of good and evil as principles. We cannot help asking what are the consequences of these principles. Will righteousness be vindicated, approved, sustained? Will sin be judged, condemned, destroyed? Our Lord answers that question. He says the Paraclete will convince the world of judgment. To a certain extent this had been done before. "Whatsoever a man

* Rom. iv. 25.

soweth that shall he also reap," was a law
written on man's nature and illustrated in all
his history. But here it is proved by the judgment of the Prince of this world. He was
judged by the victory of Christ in the wilderness.
He was judged by the expulsion of demons from
the bodies and the souls of men. When the
seventy returned to their Master and told Him
how these evil powers were subject to them in
His name, He gave the meaning in the words:
"I beheld Satan fallen as lightning from
heaven." * And so, when the shadow of the
cross was falling over Him, He could say, "Now
is the judgment of this world; now shall the
Prince of this world be cast out." † And,
assuredly, if He conquered in the wilderness,
He achieved a yet more splendid victory in the
garden and on the cross. And, if the power of
sin was broken by the sacrifice of the cross, the
victory was completed and the triumph was
celebrated by the resurrection from the grave,
by the ascension into heaven, and by the coming
of the Holy Ghost. Well might He, then, the
Guide into all truth, bring home to the hearts of
men the conviction that the Prince of this world
is judged.

* S. Luke x. 17, 18.
† S. John xii. 31.

Such was the preparatory work which the Holy Spirit had to perform in the world, before men could become deeply conscious of the evil from which they needed to be delivered. But it was only a preparation for that union with the second Adam by which alone the new life of grace could be realized and maintained ; and it is the work of the Holy Spirit to bring about that union, and to make it effectual by the stirring up of the new life in the soul, and by fostering its growth and development. Thus we are led to consider the beginning of the spiritual life in the new birth.

iv. SPIRITUAL BIRTH.—The word Regeneration (*Palingenesia*) occurs only twice in the New Testament : once in S. Matt. xix. 28 ("In the regeneration, when the Son of man shall sit in His glory "), and again in Titus iii. 5 ("He saved us through the washing [or laver] of regeneration, and renewing of the Holy Ghost.") In the former passage the allusion is to the "times of restoration of all things" ;* in the latter, to Holy Baptism. S. John makes the largest use of this idea ; but the same thought, with somewhat different application, is found in S. Paul and S. Peter.† The classical text on the subject is, of course, S. John iii. 5, in which are contained the

*Acts iii. 21. †1. Cor. iv. 14. 1. S. Peter i. 23.

words of our Lord: "Except a man be born of water and the Spirit, he cannot enter into the Kingdom of God."

It is almost unnecessary to remark that fierce controversies have raged around these words, into the smoke and dust of which we shall enter no further than by making two remarks. In the first place, the text was originally understood to refer to Baptism. As Hooker remarks, in reference to the Puritans of his day, "they cunningly affirm that 'certain' have taken those words as meant of material water, when they know that of all the ancients there is not one to be named that ever did otherwise either expound or allege the place than as implying external baptism." * The other remark is this, that nearly all the Reformed Confessions of the sixteenth and seventeenth centuries teach the doctrine of Baptismal Regeneration. We may then proceed to clear up the meaning of this New Birth in the light of Scripture and experience ; and to ask how spiritual life originates in man.

We have already pointed out that this life is in Christ, the Second Adam, in whom the human race found a new Head and a new Root. In all that He did, Christ stood for the race

* Ecclesiast. Polity v. 59 (3.)

whose representative He was. When He died,
all died, as S. Paul declares: " We thus judge
that one died for all, therefore all died."* So
when he rose, all rose. He was "raised again
for our justification."† The resurrection of
Christ was the regeneration of mankind in Him,
the Head and Representative of men. Thus S.
Paul declares that the resurrection of Christ was
His new birth: "God hath fulfilled the same
unto our children, in that He raised up Jesus ; as
also it is written in the second Psalm : "Thou art
My Son ; this day have I begotten Thee." ‡ And
this again is applied by S. Peter § to those who
are represented by Christ. For he tells us that
God, "according to His great mercy, begat us
again unto a living hope by the resurrection of
Jesus Christ from the dead." Thus the resurrection of Christ was the new birth of mankind.
But how, then, is this new life to be communicated to individual men and women ? The answer is not difficult. Our Lord, when He
ascends into heaven, leaves behind on earth, as
His representative, as the depository of His
grace, His mystical Body, the Church. And
this was really a new creation. For the first
time there was on earth a Body, knit to God

* II. Cor. v. 14.   † Rom. iv. 25.
‡ Acts xiii. 33.   § I. S. Peter i. 3.

in Jesus Christ by the bonds of a supernatural
life, a Body which could be designated by names
of such dignity as had never before been conferred upon any community : the Family of God,
the mystical Body of the Lord Jesus Christ, the
Temple of the Holy Ghost. Of this Church S.
Paul says, it is "His Body, the fulness of Him
that filleth all in all." *

Now comes the question : By what means are
individuals connected with this Body. It is by
being "in Christ" that one becomes "a new
creature." † By what means is this new creation
accomplished ? The instrumental cause is Baptism and the Word, the receptive or conditioning
cause is Faith, but the efficient cause is the Holy
Spirit of God. When difficulties are raised as
to the connection of spiritual blessings with
material instrumentality, it should be remem-
bered that the Church itself, into which we are
baptized, is a material thing ; and if the characters and designations of the Church are remem-
bered, the doubts as to the privileges into which
we are admitted by Holy Baptism will come to
an end.

No one hesitates to admit that Baptism is the
door of the Church, and most will admit that
the baptized are brought into covenant with

* Ephes. i. 23.   † 2 Cor. v. 17.

God; but whether we think of the nature and blessings of the covenant, or of the characters of the Church, we shall find a justification for the expressions which we employ concerning the baptized. If the Church is the Body of Christ, then may we say that in Baptism we are made members of Christ. If the Church is the Family of God, then may we say that in Baptism we are made children of God. But the Agent in this great transaction is the Holy Spirit of God. It matters little whether we speak of our adoption into the Family, or of our regeneration, the beginning of our participation in a new life, or of our grafting into the Body of Christ. It is the change which is effected in our passing from membership in the Old Adam to membership in the new, from a state of nature to a state of grace; and it is effected by the Holy Spirit.

When our Blessed Lord went down to the River Jordan to be baptized, the heavens opened, and the Spirit of God rested upon Him, anointing Him for His work, And it is this Holy Dove Who now truly, although invisibly, hovers over each baptismal font, and gives efficacy to the rite which is not the act of man, but of God. In this regard it is sufficient merely to note some of the Scripture references. The passage already mentioned, as occurring in the third chapter of

S. John's Gospel, will occur to all; and also the
words of S. Paul, in which he speaks of the
"laver of regeneration" and the "renewing of
the Holy Ghost"; whilst the plain language of
the same apostle equally sets before us the
agency of the Blessed Spirit in the sacrament of
Baptism : "In one Spirit were we all baptized
into one body, whether Jews or Greeks, whether
bond or free; and were all made to drink of one
Spirit." *

V. SPIRITUAL LIFE AND GROWTH.—But here
we must carefully note the connection between
spiritual birth and spiritual life, and so, perhaps,
remove some difficulties experienced in regard
to what is called Baptismal Regeneration. In
one sense, the act of Regeneration in Holy Baptism is complete. The new Branch is really
grafted into the vine : the child of man is truly
adopted into the Family of God : the member of
Adam has been made a member of Christ. But
in another sense the act is continuous. The
Word must give efficacy to the element of
water, and the principle of Faith is a condition
for the full communication to the heart of that
life which is the gift of the Holy Ghost. Christ
sanctifies and cleanses the Church not only "by
the washing of water," but also "with the

* 1 Cor. xii. 13.

Word"; * and S. Peter declares that Christians are " begotten again, not of corruptible seed, but of incorruptible, through the Word of God, which liveth and abideth." † And we know that neither the Word nor the water can profit unless "they are united by faith with them that hear." ‡ And so, again, this faith is inseparably connected with the presence of the Holy Ghost, Who is, on the one hand, the cause of Faith, since " no man can say, Jesus is Lord, but in the Holy Spirit"; § whilst, on the other hand, His presence is the response to the prayer of faith, since our heavenly Father gives " the Holy Spirit to them that ask Him." ‖ He is also the security of our new life. " Having believed, ye were sealed with the Holy Spirit of promise."¶

It is apparent that when S. John, in his first epistle, + speaks of those who are " born of God," he is referring, not simply to those who have been baptized, but to those in whom the new life has taken effect, and so is manifested in faith and love. But however we may understand the meaning and effect of the Divine act which is described as regeneration, begotten again, or born again, whether as being complete in the

---

* Ephes. v. 26.   † 1 S. Peter i. 23.
‡ Heb. iv. 2.   § 1 Cor. xii. 3.
‖ S. Luke xi. 13.   ¶ Ephes. i. 13.   + iii. 9 : iv. 7, etc.

Sacrament of Baptism, or whether as continued
by the power of the Gospel, or whether, as some
have done* who have fully received the doctrine
of the Church, we refer to the turning of the
soul from sin and the world to God in more
mature years; in each case it is the work of
the Holy Spirit of God.

The Spiritual life is differently designated in
the New Testament. It is a life of renunciation
—the renunciation of sin and the world. It is
the life of holiness and the life of love. "Whosoever is begotten of God doeth no sin." † Does
this mean that those who are alive to God are
sinless? The apostle could not mean this, for
he says the reverse : "If we say we have no sin
we deceive ourselves." But he does teach
us that the one sure sign of our being begotten
of God, of our having received of Him that new
nature which can be ours only through union
with the Second Adam and by the power of the
Holy Ghost, is our antagonism to evil, our
hatred of sin, our refusal to consent to it as the
law of our life.

This is what we call a negative evidence of
the new life; but there is one principle which

---

* e. g. Lacordaire ; Fragment appended to his *Lettres à
des jeunes gens*.

† 1. S. John, iii. 9.

is positive and which is indispensable, without which there can be no true life in the soul—it is the principle of love. "Love is of God," says S. John, * "and every one that loveth is begotten of God, and knoweth God. It could not be otherwise. God is Love. His very Being is Love; and every one who partakes of the life of God must also love. It is the teaching which pervades the whole of the first epistle of S. John. "We love, because He first loved us." "We know that we have passed out of death into life, because we love the brethren."† But S. Paul is no less decisive and emphatic. We may have great gifts, he says, and large knowledge, and strong faith, but if ye have not love, we are "nothing"; ‡ and of the three graces which remain and never pass away, the greatest is Love. The presence of the Spirit of love in the heart, love to God and to man, is the one evidence of the life of God in the soul of man.

There is one point which here demands special consideration. If we are guided by the analogy of the spiritual life to the natural, we shall understand that life is a principle which grows, and which admits of various degrees, from the first weak beginning up to such degrees of per-

* St. John iv, 7.
† I. S. John iv. 19; iii. 14. ‡ I. Corinth. xiii. 1, 2, 13.

fection as may be possible for the creature. There are some who contend that the life of holiness is here complete; but we must be careful in our use of such language. It is true, indeed, that we are complete, made full in Him "who is the Head of all principality and power";* but there is nothing in Scripture or in Christian experience which teaches the necessity or the fact of personal perfection in the disciples of Jesus Christ here on earth. S. Paul declared that he had not "already obtained," nor was he "already made perfect."† It is the work of the ministry, it is the aim of the Christian, to foster and attain to "the knowledge of the Son of God," so that we may come, in due time, "unto a full-grown man, unto the measure of the stature of the fulness of Christ." ‡

The life of Grace, then, is a state of progress and growth; and there is need of the work of the Blessed Spirit throughout its whole course and development. The principle of love is in the heart, and with this there is the unreserved consecration of the will to God. This is a true and necessary beginning, but it is no more. It may seem very simple to go on from such a beginning. "Love," says Augustine, "and do what thou wilt." Yes, what thou wilt, when

* Coloss. ii. 10.   † Phil. iii. 12.   ‡ Ephes. iv. 13.

animated by the Spirit of love ; but there is much
that hinders and chills and depresses our love :
and it needs to be nourished and strengthened
and reanimated by the Spirit of love ; and we
have to wrestle against principalities and powers
and run with patience the race that is set before
us. This, then, is the work of gradual sanctification, the enthroning of the Spirit of God, the
Spirit of love, with ever increasing authority and
power, in the heart and will, until He has perfect
dominion over all the forces of our nature,
beating down all those tendencies which naturally resist His influence, forming and strengthening
habits in accordance with the spirit of love, and
moulding the whole character into conformity
with the character of Christ. Such is the work
of sanctification, such is the nature of spiritual
growth, and it is, from beginning to end, the work
of the Holy Ghost, "the Lord and Giver of life."

In the work of Sanctification the Holy Spirit
makes use of Divine ordinances ; and here there
is a danger in two different directions. In the
use of these ordinances some are tempted to forget that they are but means of grace, whilst
others are, for this reason, disposed to neglect
them or even to despise them. Thus with the
one class the Bible and Prayer and the Sacrament
of the Body and Blood of Christ are used in a

mechanical kind of a way, as though the mere reading of the Scriptures, the mere saying of prayers, and mere reception of Holy Communion worked in the soul all the salutary effects that would promote the growth in grace. It is impossible to deny that there is here a very real danger, and that we need to be put on our guard against it.

But the danger of neglecting ordinances and of thinking we may become partakers of all divine blessings by the agency of the Holy Spirit, without any regard to the means of grace is hardly less considerable. The Scriptures are both the utterances of those who spoke as they were moved by the Holy Ghost, and they are the weapons which He wields in carrying on the warfare against evil.

The "Sword of the Spirit" is "the Word of God." Shall we then be really honouring the Spirit of God when we profess to depend upon His aid, and yet neglect His word? And so with all the appointed means of grace. If the ordinance of Confirmation, the Laying on of Hands, has been appointed for the assuring to us of our place in the mystical Body of the Lord and our participation in all the varied gifts of the Spirit, shall we not equally dishonor Him, if we neglect this ordinance, or, on the other hand, if we use

it in a mechanical manner without a sense of
His presence ?   And so with the supreme ordinance of the Gospel.   It is the communion of the
Body and Blood of Christ.*   Yet the blessing
comes not to those who "carnally and visibly
press with their teeth the Sacrament."†   "It is
the Spirit that quickeneth."‡   It is only as the
Holy Spirit carries on His own blessed work of
illumination, kindling, applying, nourishing, that
the blessing comes to the soul and it grows in grace.

VI. CONSUMMATION OF LIFE.—Great is the
work of the Spirit of God in bringing new life
from God to the souls of men, and in carrying
onwards the development of that life through all
the changing scenes of our earthly existence.
But there is a still more glorious future set before us, and the Holy Spirit is concerned in
its realization.   Day by day the manna falls,
and our spiritual life is renewed as we pass onwards to the Land of Promise.   But there is,
beyond, a nobler sphere for the development of
our being in that new heaven and new earth
wherein dwelleth righteousness, "in the times of
restoration of all things, whereof God spake by
the mouth of His holy prophets." §

Not once, but many times in different words,
is this hope set before us.   "The Lord Himself

* 1 Cor. x. 16. † Article 29. ‡ S. John vi. 63. § Acts iii. 21.

shall descend from heaven with a shout, with
the voice of the archangel, and with the trump
of God"; * and along with this the "dead shall
be raised incorruptible, and we shall be
changed." †   And then "the creation itself also
shall be delivered from the bondage of corruption
into the liberty of the glory of the children of
God." ‡   It is the Holy Ghost Who is the author
of this new birth of humanity and of the world.
That cleansing fire which shall descend upon
the old world of corruption, and out of which the
new world of purity and goodness shall, Phœnix-
like, arise, is the same fire which sat upon the
infant Church on the Day of Pentecost; for it is
the Holy Spirit, and He alone, Who can raise the
dead from their graves and renovate the earth
as a habitation for the redeemed; for "He that
raised up Christ Jesus from the dead shall
quicken also your mortal bodies through His
Spirit that dwelleth in you." §

Thanks be unto God for His unspeakable gift.

"Blessed be the God and Father of our Lord
Jesus Christ, Who, according to His great
mercy, begat us again unto a living hope . . .
unto an inheritance incorruptible and undefiled
and that fadeth not away." ¶

---

* 1 Thess. iv. 16.   † 1 Cor. xv. 52.   ‡ Rom. viii. 21.
§ Rom. viii. 11.   ¶ 1 S. Peter i. 3, 4.

LECTURE VII.

THE ADVOCATE.

The word Paraclete means Advocate, as applied (1) to Christ, (2) to the Holy Spirit. Christ the Advocate and Intercessor above, the Holy Ghost within. I. Our need of the intercession of the Holy Ghost. No less than of the mediation of Christ. Ignorance and weakness in prayer. 1. We know not what we should pray for. 2. We know not how to pray. ii. Here, too, an advocate with the Father. The Holy Spirit helpeth. 1. He enlightens. 2. Excites desires for heavenly things. 3. Gives confidence in prayer. 4. Gives words and thoughts and unuttered longings. Note the sympathy of the Holy Spirit with the longings of the whole creation and the regenerate spirit. iii. Benefits and blessings of this work in the heart. 1. Prayer, though unuttered, known by God. 2. Such prayer acknowledged and answered. iv. Yet other lessons. 1. Secret of neglect of prayer. 2. Secret of failures in prayer. 3. Learn where true power in prayer is to be found.

"I WILL pray the Father," said our Lord to His disciples, "and He shall give you another Comforter" *—Paraclete, Advocate. It is necessary that we should dwell upon this word for a moment, since it is understood in various senses. The word in the Greek is *Paracletos*, Paraclete, and etymologically cor-

* S. John xiv. 16.

responds with the Latin *Advocatus*, Advocate. In the New Testament it is used in two passages; first, in the valedictory address of our Lord four times, * in reference to the Holy Ghost, and once by implication to our Lord Himself; and again with direct reference to the Lord Jesus Christ, in the first Epistle of S. John : † "We have an Advocate with the Father, Jesus Christ the Righteous."

Two principal ideas have been connected with the word, the idea of advocacy and that of consolation. The Latin word Advocate represents, as nearly as possible, the Greek word Paraclete. Accordingly, in the Greek dictionaries we find the word defined, "Called to one's aid in a court of justice, *advocatus*" ; ‡ and again, "One who maintains the cause of anyone before a judge." § And thus we can at once see the fitness of its application to our Lord, since He is our Advocate before the throne of God, who ever liveth to make intercession for us. But, indeed, it is no less appropriately applied to the Holy Spirit, since He is our Advocate within our hearts, making intercession for us there, according to the will of God. ‖

* S. John xiv. 16, 25 ; xv. 26 ; xvi. 7.   † 1. S. John ii. 1.
‡ Liddell & Scott s. v.
§ "Qui causam alicujus agit coram judice."—Grimm.
‖ Rom. viii. 27.

The translators of the Authorized Version have adopted the English word "Comforter," as the representative of the Greek Paraclete; and the revisers have retained the same word, probably out of consideration for the feelings of those to whom the word had become endeared. In its original use, as a translation of the late Latin word *Confortator*, strengthener, it was perhaps a little nearer to the meaning of the Greek original; but there is now hardly a question among scholars as to the meaning of Paraclete being Advocate. *

We have no choice, then, as to the meaning of this word, and therefore no hesitation in accepting the word Advocate, instead of Comforter. Jesus Christ is our Advocate and intercessor before the throne of God, and the Holy Ghost is the Advocator or Intercessor within our hearts; and we need the one as much as we need

---

* The explanation of the ordinary translation is given very well by Godet, in his commentary on S. John (xiv. 15-17): "The term of Paracletos, literally, 'Called to one's aid.' has been taken by Origen and Chrysostum in the active sense of Comforter. Under the influence of the Vulgate * this false sense has passed into French [and English] versions. It is now recognized that the word, having a passive form, should have a passive meaning; 'One who is called as support, as sustentation.' This is exactly the meaning of the Latin term *Advocatus*, and of our word Advocate, the defender of the accused before the tribunal. Compare Bishop Westcott's Commentary *in loc.*, and Bishop Lightfoot, "On a Fresh Revision of the New Testament," p. 50.

* The French version has *Consolateur*, but the Vulgate has *Paraclitus*.

the other.   For if, on the one hand, we have no
right to draw near to the throne of the heavenly
grace but through the Blood of Jesus; on the
other hand, we have no power to pray but
through the grace of the Holy Spirit.

Here is a thought which is ever made prominent in the sacred Scriptures—the weakness,
the helplessness, the dependence of man; and
along with it, as bringing relief to us in our
need, is set forth the strength of God.   "When
I am weak," says the apostle, "then am I strong,"*
and this because the Lord Jesus had declared to
him: "My grace is sufficient for thee."   The
thought of man's weakness and imperfection is
set forth with great force in the passage in the
Epistle to the Romans, which speaks of the Holy
Spirit as an Intercessor.†

Nature is labouring and groaning in sympathy
with weak and suffering man.   Even those who
have the first fruits of the Spirit groan within
themselves.   But there is a bright hope set before them.   Creation shall be delivered from the
bondage of corruption; and even during its
state of imperfection there is a powerful help for
the children of God.   They do not sigh alone.
The Spirit helps their weakness, longs with them,
even "with groanings which cannot be uttered."

* 2 Cor. xii. 10 and 9.   † Rom. viii. 18-27.

The greatness of the privilege here described may well fill us with astonishment. If we were to take the words in Holy Scripture which tell us of God's interest in man's salvation, and translate them into ordinary language, we should almost seem to be transgressing the bounds which reverence prescribes to human thoughts and words respecting the Most High. His unfathomable love for His sinful creatures, His earnest desire for their salvation, His endeavors, repeated and various, to influence them for good, the manifold ways of blessing which He has ordained and provided, the patience and long suffering He has exercised in His dealings with them, would be startling in their reference to One Who is free from passions and emotions, did we not remember that the God of the Bible is the God and Father of our Lord Jesus Christ.

And nowhere do we more deeply feel the greatness and completeness of the work of God for man's salvation than when we consider the part sustained therein by the Holy Ghost, the Paraclete. It would appear as though it had been the purpose of God to convince us that all the three Persons in the Godhead were profoundly interested in every several act put forth for the redemption of the world. We have, indeed, a striking example of this in that office of the Holy Ghost which we are now more particularly to consider. Surely, if there was one work which did peculiarly belong to the God-man, it was the work of intercession. Yet the very word, as we have seen, which S. John employs to describe the intercession of our Lord, is the characteristic designation of the Holy Spirit. "We have an Advocate with the Father, Jesus Christ the righteous," says S. John; and our Lord, speaking of the coming of the Holy Ghost, says: He, the Father, "will send you another Advocate." So, on the other hand, while we read that Jesus Christ "ever liveth to make intercession for us," we are also told by S. Paul that the "Spirit maketh intercession for us according to the will of God."

The manner of the intercession of the Holy Spirit differs from that of our Lord, as do their different relations to the Church. Our Lord has ascended into heaven, and it is there that He makes intercession for His people before the throne of God. The Holy Spirit has come down from God, out of heaven, to dwell in the Church and in the hearts of men here on earth; and it is here on earth, and within the hearts of God's people, that He offers that intercession of which the apostle speaks. It may be as well for us to have his words before us, as they will furnish us with the guidance needed for the consideration of the whole subject.

"In like manner the Spirit also helpeth our infirmity; for we know not how to pray as we ought; but the Spirit Himself maketh intercession for us with groanings which cannot be uttered; and He that searcheth the hearts knoweth what is the mind of the Spirit, because He maketh intercession for the saints according to the will of God." * In these words we are reminded of our need of help in prayer, of the manner in which this help is afforded, and of the blessings which flow from it.

i. First, then, let us consider our need of the intercession of the Holy Spirit. Man's need of the mediation and intercession of the Lord Jesus Christ is a fundamental doctrine of the Christian faith. "No man cometh unto the Father but by" Him.† This is a prominent thought in the New Testament. But we shall not be guilty of exaggeration if we declare that the intercession of the Holy Spirit is no less necessary for us than the mediation of our Blessed Lord; and S. Paul states this necessity plainly in the words we have quoted: "We know not what we should pray for—or how to pray—as we ought." Either rendering would be correct, and both meanings

* Rom. viii. 26, 27.   † S. John xiv. 6.

are involved in the statement. Our "infirmity," our weakness, is universal, and extends to every part of our moral and spiritual life; but nowhere are we more conscious of weakness and inability than in our prayers. The disciples of Christ, during His earthly ministry, implored His aid in the fulfilment of this duty : "Lord, teach us how to pray "; and we have needs, in this respect, more and greater than can be met even by the precious words which He left as a form and model of Christian prayer. We need inward assistance, illumination, kindled desire, sustained effort, before we can offer that "supplication" which "availeth much in its working."*

It is strange and curious to consider how this sense of our helplessness and ignorance is generally brought home to us. It is not a natural endowment. When we are very young we are apt to think that we do know what we need, or at least what would do us good and bring us satisfaction. As we grow older we discover our mistake. We find out that the gratification of our desires brings little satisfaction, even of a momentary character, and none that is lasting ; and moreover, that many things which we shrank from and dreaded as evils, have turned out to be blessings in disguise and fruitful of

* S. James v. 16.

good. Nor need this surprise us, if we only remember how ignorant we are of ourselves and of the world, and how slowly we come to any real knowledge of God, and of the duties which He requires of us, and of the blessings which He provides for us.

There are two aspects of our ignorance in regard to prayer: We know not what we should pray for, and we know not how we should pray. Both of these thoughts are suggested by the words of S. Paul.

1. We know not what we should pray for. Ever since man was conscious of himself he has raised the question: "Who will show us any good?" And in his helplessness he has been led astray by many false and inadequate answers. And so one man has come to believe that his good is in pleasure; another has thought it was in power; a third in fame, and so forth. But even when we have learnt and clung to the truth that the good of man is in God, and that only by union and communion with Him can we have peace, and strength, and joy, and hope, we are still ignorant of the means by which those blessings may best be attained, and often fall into the greatest errors in regard to them.

This is true even with respect to those means which are equally ordained for all. But when

we remember that our Father in heaven, in His
love and wisdom, leads men by ways which are
widely diverse, we may judge how difficult it
must be for each one of us to discover, or even
to recognize, the way which is best suited for
him to walk in. The difficulties and sorrows
which we experience in our life on earth we are
prone to regard as so many hindrances to a perfect life, when in the Providence of God they may
be ordained as helps to growth in grace. That
sickness, that bereavement, that sore temptation, which seemed calculated to wither our
hope and root up our faith, we have afterwards
found to be a means of strength and purification,
and an incentive to make earnest endeavors
after conformity with Christ.

If, however, we are apt to err in regard to the
means by which the blessings of God are conveyed to us, we are probably more apt to form
wrong judgments in regard to the time for the
answer to prayers. We are impatient of de-
lays. Why should not our prayers be heard at
once? We seem to be asking only for that
which is in accordance with the will of God,
and He is able to answer and willing to bless.
"Tarry, thou, the Lord's leisure," says the
Psalmist; * but we imagine that our own time

* Psalm xxvii. 16.

should be the Lord's. Jacob, when he wrestled
with the angel, wanted to have the blessing at once;
yet he learnt in due time how much better it was,
and how much greater was the blessing, when it
was for a season deferred. "It is good that a man
should hope and quietly wait for the salvation of
the Lord"; * and as we learn this lesson, we
come to know still better how true it is that
"we know not what we should pray for."

2. Moreover, we know not how we should
pray. We can hardly be mistaken when we
say that this defect is more universal than the
other. Some of our wants we can hardly help
knowing, but the spirit of prayer we always
need to be taught, and this the more because of
our ignorance. Knowledge and faith are mutually
supporting. If we are ignorant of God our faith
will be weak and wavering. If we are ignorant
of ourselves and our wants, our prayers will be
uncertain, unreal, lukewarm. There are few
indeed who can look back upon the past without
feeling that they have not prayed as they ought.

If we think only of the duty of preparation for
prayer, we shall be ready to confess how far we
have come short. "Prepare your hearts unto the
Lord," † said the Prophet to the people of Israel,

---

* Lam. iii. 26.   † 1 Sam. vii. 3.

and we admit the rightness of the exhortation. Yet how rash and thoughtless have been many of our prayers! Instead of meditating deeply and thinking seriously of the awful Presence into which we are entering, of the sins which we had to confess and the weakness we had to deplore, of our need of mercy and of grace to help in our time of need, we have gone into the Divine Presence sometimes almost without the least degree of preparation, as though it were sufficient merely to assume the attitude and employ the language of devotion.

And this is true not only of the thoughtless and irreligious, of whom it might still be said that they draw nigh to God with their mouth and honor Him with their lips, while their heart is far from Him ; but also of many who are not destitute of a true faith and who are really " partakers of the Divine nature." At one time we are cold, hesitating, double-minded, so that it is difficult to say whether we have any hope in prayer at all. At another time we are so rash, impetuous, impatient, that we seem to leave nothing to the wisdom and love of God, as regards giving or withholding, but wish to decide for ourselves the kind and the manner and the time of the blessing which we seek. " We know not how to pray as we ought."

ii. But here, too, " we have an Advocate with
the Father " : the Holy Spirit "helpeth our infirmity," for He "maketh intercession for the saints
according to the will of God." The difference between the intercession of the Son and that of the
Spirit has already been pointed out. This is carried on within our hearts, whilst that of Jesus is
offered before the throne of God in heaven. As
regards its essential nature we are told that He
"helpeth our infirmity," in which it is implied that
His help is coextensive with our need. Let us,
then, consider in what His intercession consists.

1. First of all, and in the fulfilment of His
work of Teacher and Guide, the Holy Spirit enlightens the minds of the disciples of Christ, and
so makes them conscious of their needs. This
is a primary requirement in the spiritual life.
We must first have light from the Word and
from the Spirit of God. "The entrance of Thy
words giveth light," says the Psalmist.* But we
need more than the teaching of the Word: we
need spiritual cleansing and enlightenment.
And this is the work of the Holy Spirit. "The
natural man," says S. Paul,† "receiveth not the
things of the Spirit of God : for they are foolish-
ness unto him ; and he cannot know them because they are spiritually judged." All is dim-

* Psalm cxix. 130.   † 2 Cor. ii. 14.

ness and obscurity in the heart of man until the Divine Spirit shines within us, "to give the light of the knowledge of the glory of God in the face of Jesus Christ." * In His light we see light; in the knowledge of God we learn to know ourselves. Such is the beginning of the work of the Spirit in the heart of man.

2. But along with the illumination of the Spirit comes the excitation of our desires for heavenly things. The one follows close upon the other. "He teaches us," says Augustine, "that we are strangers and pilgrims, and so makes us sigh for our native land." It is not the children of this world alone who are tempted to regard the visible order of things around us as their home. Human nature, even when it has put on the regenerate life, has still a tendency to gravitate to the earth, and to forget the higher world to which our better self has its affinities. But there is One present with us and dwelling in us, who is ever ready to counteract this downward tendency. The Holy Spirit of God will not suffer us to forget that we have a better country, even a heavenly, that we are already come to the City of the living God, and that here we can find our true rest, and nourishment, and refreshment.

* 2 Cor. iv. 6.

And thus, too, He causes us to know that, however sweet and pleasant many earthly things may be, they cannot really or permanently satisfy the heart of man. These cisterns of earth are, at best, but broken cisterns, that can hold little water. The food of earth often leaves us as hungry as we were before we partook of it. Taught by the Blessed Spirit we know that the Bread of life alone can satiate our hungry souls, and the Water of life can quench our thirst. By the working of His gracious inspiration we are made to long for the good things of the Kingdom, and to cry out with the Psalmist: "Like as the hart desireth the waterbrooks, so longeth my soul after Thee, O God, My soul is athirst for God, yea even for the living God." * Taught by Him the people of God are made to hunger and thirst after righteousness, and to desire the things of God more than their "necessary food"; † and would sooner that this body of flesh and blood should pine away, and faint and die, than that their souls should be deprived of the light of God's countenance, of the joy of His salvation, of the comfort of His "refreshing grace."

3. The Holy Spirit also gives confidence in prayer. "We know not how to pray as we

* Psalm xlii. 1, 2. † Job xxiii. 12.

ought." We are told to ask in faith, nothing
doubting," otherwise we must not think that we
" shall receive anything of the Lord." * But,
alas ! how few of us attain to this spirit ! In no
respect, probably, are we more deficient than in
the spirit of loving and patient trust in God. It
is no wonder. Who are we, so poor, so base, so
mean, so earthly, that we should draw nigh to
the Holy One of Israel, that we should dare to
appear in the presence of Him who is of purer
eyes than to behold iniquity ?

It is when thoughts like these take possession
of our minds that we are made to know and feel
the exceeding grace of God our Father towards
the sinful family of man. By nature we were
indeed far off from Him, " without God in the
world." But how wonderfully and mercifully has
He changed our condition ! " We have an Advocate with the Father, Jesus Christ the righteous."
Yea, " we have boldness to enter into the holy
place by the Blood of Jesus. †" In Him " we
have boldness and access in confidence through
our faith in Him." ‡ And this privilege is assured to us by the intercession of the Holy Spirit
within our hearts. We have says, S. Paul " our
access in one Spirit unto the Father." § It is He

* S. James i. 6, 7.   † Heb. x. 19.
‡ Ephes. iii. 12.   § Ephes. ii. 18.

alone that can deliver us from the spirit of bondage in which we are by nature held; for God
sends "forth the Spirit of His Son into our hearts,
crying, Abba, Father." * It is when the love of
God is "shed abroad in our hearts through the
Holy Ghost,"† when "the Spirit Himself beareth
witness with our spirit that we are children of
God,"‡ that the holy boldness which is the privilege of the children of the Most High, awakens
within us, and we can come boldly to the throne
of grace, and lay our wants and sorrows and
sufferings at the feet of Divine love and mercy,
and ask of Him those things which are requisite
and necessary as well for the body as the soul,
with the full assurance that, if for a season He
withholds from us the actual blessings that we
pray for, it is only because He is preparing for
us something better and greater than we had
deserved or desired.

4. Again, it is the Holy Spirit who gives us
the words and thoughts, and the unuttered
longings of prayer. Sometimes He gives us
even words. If it was promised to the Apostles
that words should be given to them when they
stood up to speak for God—"I will give you a
mouth and wisdom which all your enemies shall
not be able to withstand or to gainsay "§—the

* Gal. iv. 6. † Rom. v. 5. ‡ Rom. viii. 16. § S. Luke xxi. 15.

promise must have extended to the words which
they spoke to God. Surely, if it is promised
that, inasmuch as we know not how to pray as
we ought, the Spirit will help our infirmity, we
cannot doubt that many a word uttered in
prayer to God is spoken under His guidance. If
He gives us thoughts, and we know that from
Him "all holy desires and all good counsels"
proceed, what are words but spoken thoughts?
"Open Thou my lips," says the Psalmist, "and
my mouth shall show forth Thy praise;" and
when we are taught to pray that not only the
meditations of our hearts but the words of our
mouths may be accepted with God, we are sure
that such a prayer will not be offered in vain.

But the words used by S. Paul to set forth the
intercession of the Holy Spirit are still more
full of encouragement. It would hardly meet
our needs to be told that the words of our
prayers were taught by Divine inspiration. For
oftentimes our words are poor, stammering,
feeble, uncertain; and sometimes we can hardly
find articulate expression for our thoughts at all.
We bring to God a burdened, laboring heart,
and not a fluent tongue. Are we to suppose
that we are then left to our own poor resources
in prayer? Nay, for we are told that those
longings which we cannot find words to express,

which can be uttered only in sighs and groans, are as truly the outcome of the intercession of the Spirit as the prayers which we utter in words. "The Spirit Himself maketh intercession for us with groanings which cannot be uttered."

For a moment let us pause and note, in the deep and weighty words of the apostle which lie here before us, on the one hand, a striking progress in the longings for deliverance, first in the whole creation, next in the children of God, and finally in the Divine Spirit; and, on the other, the harmony which is found in the whole universe of God. There is evil in the world, and that evil is to be done away with. There are "sufferings" in "this present time," and there is "a glory that shall be revealed"; and every. thing is tending towards this future. "The whole creation groaneth and travaileth." And not only the creation at large, "but ourselves also, which have the first fruits of the Spirit, even we ourselves groan within ourselves, waiting for our adoption, to wit the redemption of our body." But even this is not all. Not only does the regenerate man sympathize with the longings of Nature, but God Himself is found in sympathy with them. "The Spirit Himself maketh intercession for us with groanings which cannot be uttered."

These are words of awful and mysterious import. God Himself within us is entering into our
sense of need and our desires. At the root of
our prayers, even when we cannot speak what
we feel and desire, the longing of the Eternal
Spirit is going up to the Eternal Father. Even
when the words of our prayers are poor and
altogether unworthy of Him to Whom they are
offered, unworthy even to set forth the great
needs of the soul, even then, side by side with
our imperfect and faulty petitions, His perfect
prayers are ascending and entering for us as
our prayers, as His intercessions, into the ear of
Him that sitteth upon the throne. And often,
when we can only sigh and groan, under a de-
pressing sense of our unworthiness and spiritual
destitution, those very sighs which we are unable
to render by words, or even by definite thoughts,
should give occasion for encouragement and not
for despondency; for we are labouring not with
any mere human desires and feelings, but with
the desires and longings of the Eternal Spirit of
God.*   It may well be that we should find His
thoughts too great for human language, and that

* The difference between interior prayer and articulate
prayer is noted by S. Paul in another place (1 Cor. xiv. 15),
when he says, "I will pray with the Spirit, and I will pray
with the understanding also."

the heart of man should labour and even faint under the weight of His Divine inspiration.

iii. But the teaching of S. Paul goes further. After speaking of our infirmity and of the gracious aid of the Blessed Spirit, he proceeds to give us further encouragement by telling us of the benefits and blessings which result from this work of the Spirit in our hearts: "He that searcheth the hearts knoweth what is the mind of the Spirit, because He maketh intercession for the saints according to the will of God." These words are full of encouragement and comfort.

1. They teach us that prayer which is true and sincere, even though unuttered, is known and understood by God. If we could only realize this principle clearly and fully, we should be delivered from serious anxieties and disappointments. Many a Christian rises from his knees feeling as though his prayers had been a mockery and his efforts well nigh fruitless. He tried to pray and he believes that he has failed. He meditated on the love of God the Father, on the intercession of the Divine Son, even on the promised aid of the Blessed Spirit. He thought of his sinfulness and weakness, of his need of mercy and grace, and he could not put his longings into form. No words would come, hardly could he even think his wants, and his

labor seemed all in vain. The Apostle tells him
that it was not in vain. God does not need words,
He can read the heart. In those groanings which
cannot be uttered He recognizes the intercession
of the Holy Spirit; and He who searches the
heart knows what is the mind of the Spirit
without any interpretation of ours.

And here, whilst we are finding comfort in
these words of S. Paul, should we not remind
ourselves of the danger which lies in the opposite
direction?   How apt we are to be contented with
our prayers merely because they seemed to flow
easily from our lips! Are we sure that such
superficial fluency was always a sign of a heart
deeply moved, deeply in earnest? Who knows
but that often such prayers have been less
acceptable to God than many a half uttered cry
or stifled groan that came from a heart in which
the Comforter was making intercession?   Let us
not regret that our "words are few," but that
our hearts are cold. He who searcheth the
heart knoweth what is in the heart. Let the
Spirit only teach us, and He who knows the
mind of the Spirit will hear the prayer which
He inspires.

2. But such prayer is not only known, it is also
acknowledged and answered. The Spirit, we
are told, "maketh intercession for the saints,

according to the will of God." Consider for a
moment what is involved in these words. What,
let us ask, is the one essential requirement in
prayer, in order that it may be acceptable? This,
pre-eminently, that it shall be according to the
will of God; for we have the testimony of S.
John: "This is the boldness which we have
toward Him, that if we ask anything according
to His will, He heareth us." * If our prayers
were inspired by our own wisdom or knowledge,
we could not be sure that they would be heard,
because they might not be according to the will
of God. But they proceed from a higher source,
even from the Spirit of God. And this intercession must be according to the will of God, for He
is God. And this is the ground of our comfort and
hope in prayer that, when we have sought the
help and guidance of the Holy Ghost, our
prayers have not been our own, but His; and
that our Father in heaven has looked not upon
our human infirmity, ignorance, wilfulness, but
upon those holy desires which he has excited
within us; and that when He looks upon them,
He will answer them. Many and great, then,
are the encouragements by which we are sustained in our approaches to the throne of grace.

* 1 S. John v. 14.

iv. But we must not forget that there are other lessons to be learnt from the words which we have been considering. And among these that we may discover the secret of our neglect of prayer. Few Christians will venture to maintain that their prayers have been as regular, as earnest, as persevering as they might have been, as they should have been. Most of us will confess that our failures in duty, our slight progress in the Divine life, our backslidings in the way of righteousness have been, for the most part, the consequence of our partial neglect of prayer. And chief among the reasons for such neglect we must place our forgetfulness of Him who maketh intercession for us, our failure to recognize His presence and grace. If the power of the Holy Spirit were strong within us, we could not help praying, for He is a Spirit of grace and supplication. Prayer would be as natural to us as speech to the child who comes near to an earthly parent.

So, also, we may find here the secret of our failures in prayer. There are two reasons for such failure. We have not, because we ask not, or because we ask amiss. And whence this defect in our prayers? Because we know not how we should ask as we ought. But this is not all. There is a way of overcoming this defect. The

Spirit helpeth our infirmity. Well, then, if we are not helped, if we go on asking for wrong things and in wrong ways, it must be because we have failed to have recourse to the one sufficient Helper, Advocate, Intercessor. Either we have grieved Him by our sinfulness, or we have quenched Him by our worldliness, or we have by our distrust or neglect deprived ourselves of the help which He was ready to give. And so our prayers have been our own and not His; and when God searched our hearts, He found not there the fruits of the presence of the Spirit, and so our prayers have failed of success.

Let us learn, then, where our true power is to be found, and whence we may obtain the strength whereby we may draw nearer to God with reverence and fear. If we are weak and powerless, God is strong, and His strength is made perfect in weakness. And the Spirit, whom He has promised, is not far off. We need not ascend to heaven to bring Him down, for He is nigh unto us and even within us, not waiting for our seeking, but anticipating and arousing our desires.

Surely, then, we may have great boldness and confidence in prayer. "Only God," it has been said, "can satisfy God." This is true of the sacrifice which is offered for the sin of the

world ; and it is equally true of the prayers
which seek for a blessing from above.   But God
can satisfy God.   The Blood of Jesus Christ
cleanseth us from all sin, and the Holy Spirit of
God maketh intercession for the saints according to the will of God.   And hence it is that
without presumption we may "come boldly to the
throne of grace," and pray without fear or doubting, and "receive mercy and may find grace to
help us in time of need."*

* Heb. iv. 16.

LECTURE VIII.

THE INNER WITNESS.

Speculative studies become practical. The doctrine of the Holy Spirit near to man's experience. The witness of the Spirit. I. Difficulties to be surmounted. Two Points to be made clear. 1. The witness of the Spirit to man's adoption by God is desirable and obtainable. Such assurance gives definiteness and energy. Personal belief not sufficient. The Holy Spirit a perfect witness. 2. Yet assurance not a necessary part of faith. II. The nature and manner of the testimony. It is testimony to a present relationship. It is the testimony of the Holy Spirit with the Spirit of man. The Spirit of adoption, crying, Abba, Father. III. Yet this testimony should be verified. Where the Spirit is, there is the fruit of the Spirit. 1. Truth. 2. Love. 3. Sacrifice. 4. Heavenly Spirit. A pledge of future Glory.

There are very few subjects of study which are of merely speculative interest. Even although, at first sight, this might seem to be the reverse of the truth, a deeper investigation will convince us that it rests upon a sure foundation of experience. Even those sciences which at one time seemed to have little connexion with the practical life of man, have now declared their power of ministering to every day activity. For example, Metaphysic, which was once supposed to dwell in the clouds, now stands at our doors:

Astronomy, which, at one time, was claimed as his own by the charlatan, has now become a guide for every day work.

But if this can be said of those sciences which seem the furthest removed from man's daily life, what shall we say of those which deal with the very springs of human thought and action? Of the science of man and the science of God? Of the supreme science in which all sciences find their centre, the science of Theology? And yet, for all this, there are human beings who will read about religion, and talk about religion, and argue about religion, without for one moment concerning themselves about their own relation to the Most High. There are many who are, professedly at least, worshippers in our sanctuaries and hearers of the Word of God, who hardly concern themselves with the question: What is their place in the family of God?

But this question is brought home to us with greater force when we are thinking of the Holy Spirit of God—not so much of the absolute God Who dwells in the high and lofty place, or of the manifested God in the person of Jesus Christ, but of God abiding in us, dwelling in our hearts, Who is present to make all that Christ has done effectual for us. Surely it is impossible for us to meditate on the work of the Third Person of the

Holy Trinity without considering what part we ourselves may have in His work. It is He who grafts us into the Body of Christ and makes us to live in Him; and it is He who gives the assurance that we have not received His grace in vain. "The Spirit Himself beareth witness with our spirit that we are children of God." Here is a means for putting an end to our doubts, final and unquestionable, the testimony not of our own hearts only, or of our fellow-man, but of God.

Now, it is easy to see, when we approach a subject of this kind, dealing at once with the mysteries of spiritual experience and of Divine grace, that we encounter two different kinds of danger. On the one hand, we find a critical rationalism which would reduce the Divine to mere human states and emotions; and on the other, a mystic fanaticism which refuses any place to human judgment or reason. It is sufficient to mention these dangers that we may be on our guard, whether in our interpretation of spiritual experience or of sacred Scripture.

Then there is another kind of opposition in regard to the nature and value of the testimony here spoken of. For, while there are some who declare that the assurance produced by the witness of the Spirit is a necessary part of true faith, so that no one can be thought to have a living faith in Christ without such assurance, there are others who declare that this is undesirable and should not be sought for. It is important that these subjects should be considered and settled as far as we can do so before we proceed to consider more nearly the nature and meaning of this witness of the Spirit of which the apostle speaks.

i. These, then, are the two preliminary points for which we contend. First, that such a testimony of the Divine Spirit to our place in the Family of God is desirable and obtainable; but that, secondly, such assurance is not a necessary part of a true and living faith. We regard both of these points as of no small practical importance.

1. First, then, we assert that the inner witness of the Spirit to our Sonship to God is desirable and generally obtainable. Is it not to be desired that a man should be able to say: God is my Father and I am His child? Would any one naturally prefer a doubt on this subject to a practical certainty? On matters of quite subordinate importance we are impatient to be left in doubt. We often say, we would rather know the worst than be left in suspense, because then we should know what to do. Indeed, it is only under conditions of reasonable certainty

that we ever find strong, decisive, and vigorous action. And if this be so, in regard to the ordinary business of life, surely there is one privilege above all others, and in reference to which the greatest anxiety may be excused or even expected, the privilege of adoption into the Family of God.

There may be human beings who are indifferent to this privilege and do not concern themselves with the question. But such persons can hardly be thought reasonable. Suppose there were a young man in the midst of us whose origin was a mystery, round whom there gathered whisperings of a royal parentage and expectations of a throne. What should we say of such an one if he took no interest in such a question? Yet such a case bears no comparison to that which we are considering. Lowliness of birth might be a blessing instead of a loss. But to be a child of God or a mere son of earth, having no part in the Kingdom of blessedness—this is an alternative of the gravest import.

On such a question our personal belief and assurance will not suffice us. In every department of thought and life men seek to strengthen their own convictions and hopes by the testimony of others. "It is certain," says Novalis, "my conviction gains infinitely the moment another soul believes in it." Mahomet never forgot the trust of his wife, Kadijah, and her faith in his mission. "She believed in me," he said, "when none else would believe." * Few of us are without some experience of convictions deepened and strengthened and of hopes brightened by the comforting testimony of a friend or a counsellor.

But the value of such a testimony must be determined largely by the character of the witness. A flatterer, a self-seeker, or even a thoughtless or partial friend will not count for much. We must be satisfied of the sincerity and moral weight of him who offers the testimony. And what a witness God has provided for us! The Christian's co-witness is no other than God Himself. The Spirit, the Holy Spirit of God, God the Holy Ghost, Himself beareth witness with our spirit that we are children of God.

But our heavenly Father, in providing such testimony, has declared that it is desirable and attainable. It can only be the abuse of the doctrine which has led to a doubt on this subject. Men destitute of humility, full of spiritual pride, may have caricatured the confident, yet always humble and reverent language of the sacred writers. But that can be no reason for denying

* Carlyle, "The Hero as Prophet."

the reality of a privilege which God has provided
for us.   There may be many degrees of clearness in the assurance of our place in the family
of God ; but the privilege is one to which we
may lawfully aspire and which we may fitly
exercise.

We behold examples of such assurance in the
New Testament. " We have left all and followed Thee," said S. Peter. Was there any
doubt in his mind as to the reality of his choice ?
" Thou knowest all things," he said again ;
" Thou knowest that I love thee."   He knew
that the eye of Christ could see nothing but true
and fervent devotion to Himself in the heart of
His disciple.*   And so S. Paul shows the same
undoubting assurance in regard to his own faith
and his relation to his Master.   " I know whom
I have believed, and I am persuaded that He is
able to guard that which I have committed unto
Him against that day "; and again : " I have
fought the good fight, I have finished the course,
I have kept the faith; henceforth there is laid
up for me the crown of righteousness, which the
Lord, the righteous Judge, shall give to me at
that day." †   It is true that these utterances
belong to the last days of the apostle's life, and
express a greater ardor of hope than his earlier

* S. Matt. xix. 27 ; S. John xxi. 17.   † Tim. i. 12 ; iv. 8.

writings, but in these also there is always present a calm, settled assurance of his place in the Kingdom of Christ, in the Family of God. Now, in this respect the apostles had no privileges which are not equally provided for all Christians, and there is no reason why every faithful disciple of Jesus Christ should not have the inward experience of Peter and of Paul.

2. Whilst, however, we would earnestly assert the reality of such testimony, we would, with equal energy, protest against the notion that there can be no true faith in the heart which has not a full consciousness of adoption into the Family of God. Such an assurance is not required as a condition of salvation by our Lord Jesus Christ or His representatives. The only thing which is necessary to salvation is the life of God in the soul of man, and the only necessary evidence of its existence is a faith that works by love.

Many of the most devout, loving, faithful of men have been harassed and tormented by doubts of their acceptance of God, when those who knew them best were fully convinced that there could be no doubt on the subject. One of the most remarkable examples of the kind is that of Cowper, the poet, a man so absolutely submitted to the will of God that he could himself declare that he was not conscious of a rebellious thought, and yet never seemed able to enter into the "liberty of the children of God." If, therefore, such doubts should sometimes beset us, we shall do well to seek deliverance from them, the deliverance provided by the Divine Spirit; but even if the actual internal assurance of Sonship should, for a time, be withheld, we may yet have something of the witness of the Spirit, as will appear when we consider the nature and manner of His testimony.

ii. To these points we must now turn our attention; and first, let us note the fact to which the Spirit bears witness—"that we are children of God"; and here let us particularly remark, it is a present relationship to which the Holy Ghost bears witness.

It is quite common to hear the assurance wrought in the heart by the inspiration of the Holy Spirit spoken of as though it were the confidence of future and final salvation. We need not stop to ask here how far or in what circumstances such an assurance may be obtained. This, at least, is not the subject of the apostle's testimony in the passage to which we have referred. The apostle is here speaking of a testimony not to any future state or condition, however intimately that future may be connected

with the present, but to a present fact, namely,
an actual filial relationship to Almighty God.
"The Spirit Himself," he says, "beareth witness
with our spirit, that *we are* children of God."
He bears witness that the work of grace has been
begun in us, that there is within the soul a new
spiritual life, higher in origin and character than
the life of nature. He declares that we have
now a right to say "Our Father," that we have
now boldness to enter into the holiest of all, that
we are actually members of a society which is
not of earth but of heaven, and that we are
citizens of the heavenly city, the new Jerusalem, and not merely children of the family of
man. Such, then, is the nature, the content of
the testimony which the Spirit bears within the
regenerate heart. But there is a question
closely connected with this which demands consideration : In what manner is this testimony
given ? And in answering this question we
must follow the guidance of the Apostle, who
tells us that the "Spirit Himself beareth witness
with our spirit." Let us mark the form of the
phrase. It is not in our spirit or to our spirit,
but with our spirit; so that the testimony of
the Spirit of God and of the Spirit of man with
reference to this fact is one testimony, one single
utterance, so to speak, although there are two

distinct agents uniting in the utterance. It is something not consciously distinguishable from the voice of our own spirit, the experience of our own heart.

This remark is of more importance than might at first sight appear. Persons have often dis_ quieted themselves without cause, because they were not conscious of a testimony to their adoption into the family of God distinct from the sense of sonship which arose within their hearts and prompted them to throw themselves upon the love of our Father in heaven. Along with this personal assurance, which seemed to belong to themselves, they expected to receive and to experience something which did not in the same way belong to themselves. They longed to hear a voice from heaven, to have the sense of a mysterious contact with another world, such as they might attribute to an external and superior power and influence.

It is clear that this is not the meaning of the Apostle's words. The Holy Spirit is undoubtedly declared to be present in and with the spirit of the child of God; but the testimony which He communicates is not distinct from that which arises within the regenerate spirit itself. He is the Life of our life, the Spirit of our spirit, the Living Power which imparts all spiritual vision,

which stirs up every holy emotion, which
fashions every noble purpose; but these acts He
performs in union with the spirit which He has
quickened and in which He dwells. "The
Spirit Himself beareth witness with our spirit
that we are children of God." Consequently the
sense of sonship which arises in the heart of man
is by S. Paul attributed at one time to the human
spirit, at another to the Divine. In the verse
preceding the one now specially before us he
says: "Ye received not the Spirit of bondage
again unto fear; but ye received the spirit of
adoption, whereby we cry Abba, Father." He
then adds the words we have been considering,
testifying to the co-operation of the Divine Spirit,
whilst in his Epistle to the Galatians (iv. 6) he
presents the other side of the complete truth:
"Because ye are sons, God sent forth the Spirit
of His Son into your hearts, crying, Abba,
Father." This, then, is the witness of the Spirit
with our spirit, the sense of God's fatherly love
shed abroad in our hearts, the longing for communion with Him, the impulse which bids us
throw ourselves at His feet in penitence, in faith,
in love; which bids us cry out, Abba, Father,
and so claim for ourselves an interest in His
mercy, His grace, and in all that is His.

When such a voice is heard, it affords a presumption that it brings the testimony of the Holy Spirit. The spirit of heathenism is a spirit of abject fear. The Pagan does not dare to draw near to his god without first endeavouring to appease his wrath. He has not the spirit of adoption. Neither has the Hebrew. The spirit of Judaism is a spirit of bondage. The Israelite is still only a servant, not a son; for the Law could not give him the liberty of the child. Only the Spirit of Christ is the Spirit of adoption; and the sense of sonship is the effect of His presence. Where, therefore, the spirit of sonship is found, there is good reason to believe that God is sealing us for His own, and giving us the earnest of the Spirit in our hearts.*

iii. But here we are met with the charge of fanaticism. We are told that we are making the assurance of adoption into the family of God to depend upon the state of a man's feelings; or, at least, we are making these feelings a certain evidence of His adoption. Such a course, it is urged, is unwise and dangerous, for it is most certain that men do continually deceive themselves as to their state before God. Such cautions are not unneeded, and in any case we shall feel bound, at this point, to indicate the

* 2 Corinth. i. 22.

limitations and qualifications of the testimony of
which we have been speaking.

The evidence of our heart—let us freely admit
it—is not always true. The Spirit which beareth
witness with our spirit may possibly be a spirit
of error and falsehood, and not a spirit of truth.
Satan sometimes transforms himself into an
angel of light in order to deceive the children of
men. He might even produce in the minds of
his own children the conviction that they were
the children of God. Some who boasted themselves as children of Abraham were solemnly
warned by our Lord that they had no claim to
this designation, and were, in truth, children of
the evil one. It is, therefore, obvious that the
mere feeling or sense of sonship cannot be relied
upon, unless it is corroborated by other circumstances.

The difficulty of such verification, however,
is only apparent. Apart from the difficulty in-
herent in all moral judgments, there is really no
reason for regarding the solution of this question
as peculiarly arduous. There is one thing especially to be had in remembrance which will
make the whole subject comparatively easy.
The witness here borne is the witness of the Holy
Spirit present within the heart, and where He
dwells there must be found the fruits of the

Spirit. Let these points be carefully and clearly kept in mind. Unless the Spirit of God is dwelling in the heart, the testimony of the heart cannot be His. But, on the other hand, if He is so dwelling in the heart, He must bring other gifts than the sense of sonship : the "fruit of the Spirit" must be there. The reality of our adoption into the Family of God, the truth of filial relation to the Most High, must be attested by the presence of the Holy Spirit, and where He dwells there must be the impress of His character, the fruits of His presence and agency.

We should here be entering upon a large subject, did we follow it up in all its bearing. "The fruit of the Spirit," says S. Paul,* " is love, joy, peace, long-suffering, kindness, goodness, faithfulness, meekness, temperance." Where these. are found, there is found the grace of the Spirit. We may, however, with advantage limit our field of observation. The Holy Spirit is pre-eminently a Spirit of truth, of love, of sacrifice, of holiness; and if He has shed abroad His grace in our hearts, then He must have diffused His light, and love, and power within us. It will be well for us to consider these points in detail.

1. The Holy Spirit, we say, then, is a Spirit of

---

* Gal. v. 22. Compare Ephesians v. 9.

truth. It is one of the special designations by
which our Lord describes Him again and again
in His great valedictory discourse. " When He,
the Spirit of truth, is come," He says, * and
and again ; " Even the Spirit of truth, whom the
world cannot receive." † And He promises that
the Spirit will guide them "into all the truth."
The Spirit who beareth witness, then, is a Spirit
of truth. Let us consider what this involves.
Surely, first of all, that if we are dwelt in by
this Spirit, we must know ourselves, our sinfulness, our weakness, our imperfections, our needs.
The Blessed Spirit convinces the world of sin, of
righteousness, and of judgment ; and so when
His light shines into our minds, we must needs
come to know our sinfulness, when He touches
the heart and the conscience, there must arise
the sense of evil and the longing for pardon. It
is impossible that the soul should not seek the
mercy which falls from the cross and the grace
which descends from our ascended Lord.

Here, then, is a primary test of the working
of the Spirit of truth in our hearts, that we
should have become conscious of our need of
redemption, and should have longed for pardon
and reconciliation. We dare not say that
such an experience is conclusive as to our

* S. John xvi. 13. † S. John xiv. 17.

relation to God. Many, it may be feared, have
gone thus far without attaining to the fullness
of the Divine life. Yet, as far as it goes, it must
be taken as an evidence of the working of the
Spirit of God. But more is needed before we
can believe that the Spirit dwells within us as a
spirit of life and sonship.

2. Further, the Spirit of God is a spirit of
love. Here we are going deeper, for this is
indeed the very root of the matter. We are
declaring the very essence of the Divine character. God is Love ; and the Holy Spirit is God,
and therefore Love.

> " Thy blessed unction from above,
> Is comfort, life, and fire of love."

Wherever the Holy Spirit dwells the spirit of
love must radiate from Him upon all around.
He is a "consuming fire," and He is perpetually
going forth to purify or destroy, and to purify
by destruction. It is He who reveals to us the
love of God in Christ. "The love of God hath
been shed abroad in our hearts through the Holy
Ghost, which was given unto us."* It is He
also who stirs within us an answering love to
God and Christ, and who brings out of that love for
the Creator a true love for the creature ; Who
makes us, in loving Him that begetteth, love

* Rom. v. 5.

him also that is begotten of Him. Wherever He dwells, hatred, and coldness, and selfishness must disappear, "for the fruit of the Spirit is love."

Let us, then, be well assured that no voice, speaking within the heart of man and calling God Father, can, in the fullest sense of the word be true, unless it comes from a heart which has learnt to love God, and Christ, and our fellow-men. Do you believe that God has sent forth the Spirit of His Son into your heart, crying, Abba, Father? We will not cast doubt upon such a testimony. But if the Holy Spirit has thus borne witness within any of us, He has done more than this; He has also stirred up thoughts of thankfulness and love, and He has begotten sentiments towards our fellow-man, if not of complacency and satisfaction, yet of compassion, and patience, and mercy, and has excited the desire to bless them, strengthen them, comfort them.

3. Yet, perhaps, even here we may demand an additional evidence of reality. Benevolent and affectionate sentiments are sometimes the product of nature, and, as such, are shallow and evanescent. Such sentiments must at least be tested before we can assign to them a higher origin. And in thus speaking we have no wish to throw

needless suspicion upon them. But love rejoices
to be proved, rejoices to find occasion for demo-
strating its reality and its power. And therefore
we must take note that the Spirit of God, the
Spirit of love, is essentially a Spirit of Sacrifice.
This character of the Holy Spirit and of the love
of God is everywhere manifested in the Divine
revelations to mankind. This is a deep mystery ;
and he who ventures into those depths should
remember the warning words : "I speak as a
man." But Holy Scripture evidently intends
us to understand that the love of God was a love
of sacrifice. God "spared not His own Son,"
and therefore He spared not Himself. There
was sacrifice on the part of the Father. The
whole manifestation of the Son was one continued
sacrifice—in His Incarnation, in His life, in His
sufferings, in His death. The Holy Spirit was
the power in which He offered that sacrifice ;
and the same character belongs now and always
to the work of the Holy Spirit of God.

Where, therefore, the Holy Spirit dwells, there
we must find the Spirit of sacrifice. It is one of
the surest signs of a Divine indwelling and life.
Where the Spirit of sacrifice is not, God is not.
When it is and where it is under the guidance of
the principle of love, there God truly and surely
is dwelling. There is no higher test than this,

there is none which it is more necessary to apply. It is not that we should be eager to throw suspicion upon the experience of peace and joy and hope to which men lay claim. We should be slow to suggest that it is the outcome of self-deception or enthusiasm. Nor must we lightly speak of the inner joys of others as a mere sentimental religion which has no value. If religion must be practical, there is a sense in which it must also be sentimental. But if our love for God is sincere, we should not shrink from this test; and if the Spirit of God, which is the spirit of sacrifice, dwells in us, then we need have no fear of it.

If it be said that we have here a weapon that has slain its thousands, the answer is very simple. It has slain none but those who were marked for slaughter, it has slain none who ought to have been kept alive. A false hope is an evil which should be cut down and rooted out; for until this is done, a true hope cannot live and grow. It is well for us, at any cost, to know truly what we are. And one thing stands out clear in the apostolic testimony, confirmed by reason and conscience alike: "If any man hath not the Spirit of Christ, he is none of His."* But, on the other hand, the spirit of love and sacrifice is

* Rom. viii. 9.

truly the Spirit of Christ. If a man out of a loving heart, a heart that loves God because of His glory and goodness, and that so loves God that it has learnt to love men, if in the power of this love a man is willing to do and to bear and to suffer in the life of faith, then we may be well assured that the cry which comes from the heart, "Abba, Father," is a true testimony, that the Spirit which witnesseth with our spirit that we are children of God is a true spirit, even the Spirit of God and of Christ.

4. It is obvious, as already stated, that these remarks might be carried much further; but, after all, the essential truth of the matter has already been set forth. Where those characters are formed upon which we have here dilated, we are bound to attribute them to the Blessed Spirit of God, and therefore to believe that the testimony of the spirit in which he abides is a true testimony.

We will add only one other note of the Holy Spirit to those already considered. He is a heavenly Spirit, and something of the heavenly mind must belong to those in whom He dwells. Such a remark is not altogether unnecessary. There are men and women not a few who seem, in a way, religious, and yet are earthly in their thoughts and judgments. They measure men and

things by an earthly standard ; they judge actions
and events from a worldly point of view; they
weigh all things in the balances of earth. To hear
them speak, one might imagine that Jesus Christ
had never lived, or that, if He did, He was a
mere enthusiast and His life a mistake.

Well, but it may be asked : What is the
heavenly mind? It is a mind which is not
held in bondage by the things which are seen
and temporal, which carries with it the perpetual consciousness of an infinite and eternal
world above and beyond this visible and tangible world of sense. It is a mind which weighs
the things of earth in the scales of heaven,
regarding wealth, and position, and power as
gifts of God, to be used for the fulfilment of His
gracious purposes, and not for enjoyment, or
ease, or vain glory. It is a mind which views
man, and the world, and all things as in the light
of God, and lives continually as in His presence.

Such a mind will be found in those in whom the
Spirit of God has His dwelling ; and it will be well·
for all of us who claim a place in the Family of
God to consider how far it is ours. If it is, we
shall delight to meditate upon the goodness and
loving kindness of the Most High. We shall
love the Scriptures, in which are recorded His
wondrous dealings towards the children of men.

We shall value the ordinances which He has appointed as means of fellowship with Himself. The man who can say : " Lord, I have loved the habitation of Thine house, and the place where Thine honour dwelleth," " How amiable are Thy dwellings, O Lord of hosts "—that man has one more evidence that the Voice within him which cries, Abba, Father, is the voice of the Spirit of God witnessing with his spirit that he is a child of God.

We repeat, it is a thing desirable and attainable that we should thus claim our place in the Family above. If there are some who abuse this privilege and are puffed up with spiritual pride, are there not also many who deprive themselves of the peace and joy which God has prepared for them, for want of having a consciousness of their place in the Family of God? Would it not be better for them, and for us all, to be assured that we are no mere strangers and pilgrims, but fellow-citizens with the saints, and of the household of faith ? Would it not help us to fulfil all our duties to God and man more constantly, more earnestly, more cheerfully ? And as it would bring us strength in the present, so it would fill us with hope for the future; for he who can say : " Now are we the sons of God," can add, " When He shall appear we shall be like Him, for we shall see Him as He is."

NOTES

NOTE A.

Primitive Doctrine of Holy Trinity.

Some excellent remarks on this subject in Heber's "Bampton Lectures" may be quoted here: "As every innovation must have had its beginning, every religious sect its heresiarch, so will it also be allowed that the doctrine of the Trinity (if it were indeed an innovation and a heresy) must needs have been introduced, if the Apostles were still alive, in opposition to their authority; if after their decease, in opposition to the general sense of that Church which they had established . . . Whenever the innovation was effected, it must, doubtless, have had a beginning; and if that beginning had been opposed by the scholars and immediate successors of the Twelve, supported by their recent authority, the Apostles, it is plain, would not have been held in such exalted reverence by the Fathers of the succeeding age . . . The time was too short, the years were too few, the body was too extensive, for an imperceptible cause to produce effects so portentous. The corruption of

a single Church might have been effected in a few
years of neglect and ignorance ; but to pervert the
whole empire of Christ with one universal and unob-
served contagion must have required the lapse of
more than a single century .   .   .   Nor can it be
urged with any show of likelihood that, in adducing
the opinions of that body of Christians who have
agreed in the worship of a Triune Deity, we are con-
tenting ourselves with the party statements of a
single sect .   .   .   For that they to whom the titles
are applied of the Church, and the Catholic Christians were, indeed, as those names imply, the great
majority of believers, the assumption of such lofty
titles, in opposition to all who dissented from their
worship or jurisdiction, is itself no inconsiderable
argument." Ed. 2. pp. 123, 125, 129.

NOTE B.

The Sin Against the Holy Ghost.

(Consult the following passages : S. Matt. xii.
31, 32 ; S. Mark iii. 28, 29 ; S. Luke xii. 10 ; Heb.
vi. 4-6 ; x. 26, 27 ; 1 S. John v. 16.)

The three passages from the Gospels noted above
certainly refer to the same thing ; and the other
three to the same general condition. It is no wonder that commentators should have differed widely

in the interpretation of language so awful and mysterious. The offers and promises of the Gospel are so
full of grace and mercy that it must have seemed
natural and necessary to explain away warnings so
dreadful. On the other hand, the words are too
plain to admit of any softening of their awful significance by those who reverence the testimony of our
Lord.

Attempts have been made to prove that this sin
could be committed only in the time of our Lord, as
by those who regarded His miracles as being wrought
by the power of evil. Doubtless such a shocking
suggestion must have proceeded from a terribly de-
praved spiritual condition ; but this could hardly be
the essential nature of the sin. For one thing, it is
certain that the sin against the Holy Spirit is not a
mere act, but a state. No mere external act could
be unpardonable ; but there is no difficulty in im-
agining a spiritual state so debased as to admit of
no return to good.

This must be the meaning of our Lord's words
when He says that blasphemy against the Son of
man shall be forgiven, because that is a sin against
a truth or a command coming from without. But
the sin against the Spirit is an offence against the
inner Guide, and, therefore, is not a mere error, but
a wilful resistance of what is known to be good.
The sin against the Holy Ghost is, then, the continued resistance of the will of man to the voice of
God speaking in the conscience ; and he who per-

sists in such resistance becomes "guilty of an eternal sin" (S. Mark iii. 29, R.V.), for which there could not be any forgiveness, seeing that it involves final impenitence and rebellion. It is the state of those who call evil good, and good evil. It is obvious, therefore, that there can be no ground for the apprehension, found so distressing by many humble souls, that they may inadvertently have committed this terrible sin. Those who have fallen into such a condition are little likely to be troubled by their conscience. They have sinned away light and life, and are spiritually insensible and dead.

NOTE C.

The Gift of Tongues.

(Consult the following passages : Acts ii, x, xix ; 1 Cor. xiii, xiv.)

The gifts of the Holy Spirit, which accompanied the Advent of the Paraclete on the Day of Pentecost, and were continued in the Apostolic Church, were akin to the grace of the Spirit (*Charisma Charis*), but differed in this respect, that whilst grace was imparted to all believers, gifts were bestowed either upon those who possessed certain natural endowments, or upon those who were called to special work in the Church.

Among these gifts the most remarkable was the gift of tongues, as being an illustration of the power of speech, man's highest endowment, the expression of his reason. This gift, promised by our Lord, seems, at times, to have been granted momentarily to a whole community, at other times to individuals, some of whom had the power of speaking, others the power of interpreting tongues.

Various opinions have been held with reference to the exact nature of this gift. It was an opinion generally prevalent a few years ago, that those who were thus endowed were enabled to speak foreign languages, so that they were understood by men of other nationalities. Now, if we had only the second chapter of the Acts of the Apostles, or even this and the other passages relating to the gift in the same book, we might draw such an inference with great probability. But this opinion we must hold to be inconsistent with references to the gift in other passages. In the first place, there is no intimation in the New Testament that the first preachers of the Gospel were enabled to speak the languages of the peoples among whom they went to proclaim the Gospel. In the second place, S. Paul declares distinctly that, in ordinary circumstances, one speaking with tongues would be unintelligible unless there were some one to interpret (1 Cor. xiv. 2, 9, 13, 14).

We must, therefore, take the view that the tongues were the utterances of men in a state of spiritual exaltation which were understood by those who were in a similar state. These utterances were not foreign tongues, but constituted a kind of spiritual language intelligible to those under similar influences. This is the view of Meyer, De Watte, and other commentators of eminence. Dean Alford objects that such a theory is contrary to the plain language of Acts ii. 6-8, "that they spoke, and the hearers heard, in the dialects or tongues of the various peoples specified." Such an objection, we hold, cannot be sustained. The hearers did, undoubtedly, hear their own language subjectively, they understood the meaning of the utterances of those who addressed them ; but this does not necessitate the belief in a chaos of different languages actually spoken. One language was spoken, and that one language was heard as the language of all the hearers and so understood by them. Whatever difficulties may attend this view, they seem less grave than those which beset any other,

Aylwin. By THEODORE WATTS-DUNTON.

A vivid and enthralling love-story, full of movement and vigor. The tenth edition of this remarkable book is now on sale. *Crown 8vo., Cloth, $1.50; Paper, 75 cents.*

The Life and Letters of Lewis Carroll. By S. D. COLLINGWOOD, B.A.

This is the life of the author of "Alice in Wonderland." It is a work of deep interest, and the illustrations, which are reproductions of photographs, have excited great attention. *Crown 8vo., Cloth, $2.00.*

With Nansen in the North. By LIEUT. HJALMAR JOHANSEN. A record of the *Fram* expedition. With very numerous illustrations.

This is a record of Arctic experiences that cannot be read without a thrill of interest. Its characteristics are simplicity and straightforwardness. *Crown 8vo., Cloth, $1.50; Paper, 75 cents.*

The Forest of Bourg-Marie. By S. FRANCES HARRISON.

A story of French-Canadian life, which displays in a vivid and interesting manner the characteristics of the *habitant*. Its story element is strong. *Crown 8vo., Cloth, $1.25; Paper, 75 cents.*

A Sister to Evangeline: being the story of Yvonne de Lamourie. By CHARLES G. D. ROBERTS.

This work, as its name denotes, deals with the scene already made famous by Longfellow's poem. It is a most interesting story. *Crown 8vo., Deckle-edged. Cloth, gilt top, $1.50; Paper, 75 cents.*

Life of Jane Austen. By GOLDWIN SMITH, D.C.L.

The accomplished and learned author of this "Life of Jane Austen" has brought to the task a fulness of information and a literary insight that make this book a valuable addition to biography. *Crown 8vo., Library Edition, half Morocco, $1.50.*

AT ALL BOOKSELLERS, OR SENT POST-PAID BY THE PUBLISHERS

Bird Neighbors. By NELTJE BLANCHAN ; with an introduction by JOHN BURROUGHS.

Will be found not only to contain much interesting reading, but to have a high value as a work of reference. *Crown 4to, Cloth, with 52 beautiful colored photogravures, $2.25.*

Game Birds and Birds of Prey. By NELTJE BLANCHAN ; with an introduction by G. O. SHIELDS.

This book, a companion volume to the foregoing, contains the life-histories of 170 birds of prey, game-birds and water-fowl. It has 48 colored plates. *Crown 4to., Cloth $2.25.*

Christian Martyrdom in Russia : an account of the members of the Universal Brotherhood, or Doukhobortsi. By VLADIMIR TCHERTKOFF.

This is a most interesting description of the Doukhobors, our new immigrants to Canada. It contains a chapter by Tolstoy and an introduction by Prof. James Mavor. *Crown 8vo., Paper, 35 cents.*

Heart Songs. By JEAN BLEWETT.

Mrs. Blewett has taken a special place in the affections of the reading public, and this volume will undoubtedly confirm her dominion there. The predominant note of the book is buoyant optimism. *Crown 8vo., Cloth, ornamental, gilt-top, $1.00. Half Morocco, $1.50.*

A Critical Study of "In Memoriam." By the late REV. JOHN M. KING, D.D.

The wide scope of the work and its masterly dealing with the experiences of human nature give it a unique prominence in poetic literature. It will take its place not only as a text-book but as a valuable addition to private book-shelves. *Cloth, 12mo., gilt-top, deckle edges, $1.25.*

Essays on Work and Culture. By HAMILTON WRIGHT MABIE.

The place which Mr. Mabie has undoubtedly taken in modern criticism is exemplified in these books. Already he has won a large following by these delightful essays. *In eight volumes, Cloth, 12mo., gilt top, deckle-edges, $1.25 per volume.*

AT ALL BOOKSELLERS, OR SENT POST-PAID BY THE PUBLISHERS

Trimalchio's Dinner. By PETRONIUS, translated by HARRY THURSTON PECK.

This story, of the period of "Quo Vadis," brings before the reader in a realistic way, the people and the time of the reign of Nero. The book is a voice from the past. *Crown 8vo., Cloth,* $1.50 ; *Paper*, 75c.

Stories from Starland. By MARY PROCTOR, daughter of the famous astronomer.

It precisely fills the want, so often expressed, of a child's book, that is not encumbered with matters that the little reader cannot possibly understand. *Crown 8vo. Cloth,* 75c.

Cyrano de Bergerac. By EDMOND ROSTAND, a drama, translated from the French by GERTRUDE HALL.

The unanimity of the critics with regard to this piece of literary work is as surprising as it is rare. *Cloth, 16mo., with portrait of Miss Margaret Anglin as Roxane,* 50c.

Quo Vadis. By HENRYK SIENKIEWICZ, translated by JEREMIAH CURTIN.

This remarkable romance deals with the history, religion and customs of Rome in the days of Nero, which is portrayed with vividness and power. It has been called one of the greatest books of our day. *Crown 8vo. Cloth,* $1.50; *Paper,* 75c.

With Fire and Sword. By HENRYK SIENKIEWICZ.

An historical novel of Poland and Russia, authorized and unabridged edition, translated by Jeremiah Curtin, containing the history of the origin and career of the two Slav States, Poland and Russia. *Crown 8vo. Cloth,* $1.25; *Paper* 75c.

Pan Michael. By HENRYK SIENKIEWICZ, Author of "Quo Vadis," etc.

In this interesting novel, Sienkiewicz has further developed the characters and scenes to be found in "With Fire and Sword." It is characterized by great vividness and power. *Crown 8vo. Cloth,* $1.25; *Paper,* 75c.

AT ALL BOOKSELLERS, OR SENT POST-PAID BY THE PUBLISHERS

The Prisoner of Zenda. By ANTHONY HOPE, Author of " The Dolly Dialogues," etc.

" The Prisoner of Zenda " at once leaped into popularity because it brought with it a novelty and freshness that was piquant even to the most jaded novel reader. *Crown, 8vo., cloth,* $1.50. *Paper,* 75c.

To London for the Jubilee. By " KIT."

These descriptions of travel, and of a great national celebration are the best record of the ceremonies of the Diamond Jubilee, and they form a very interesting memento of the 60th year of the Queen's reign. Their gifted author had exceptional opportunities of seeing all that was going on, and the brilliant account of it that she wrote forms delightful reading. *16 mo., cloth ornamental, gilt top, 75c.; Paper, 25c.*

The Seven Seas. By RUDYARD KIPLING, Author of " Barrack Room Ballads," " The Phantom Rickshaw," etc.

These poems are among the best productions of Kipling's genius. *Crown, 8vo., cloth, ornamental,* $1.50.

The Day's Work. By RUDYARD KIPLING, Author of " The Seven Seas," etc., with eight full page illustrations.

To read this book, " The Day's Work," is to receive a mental training and nerve bracing such as must make any man or woman—and especially any young man or woman—fitter to face life and conquer it. *Crown, 8vo.; Cloth, gilt top, uncut edges,* $1.50; *Paper,* 75c.

Wolfville. By ALFRED HENRY LEWIS, illustrated by FREDERIC REMINGTON.

This is a book of fresh and quaint humor. It describes in odd, but not tedious dialect, the doings in a Western ranching settlement. The 18 illustrations by Remington are fully equal to that artist's great reputation. *Crown, 8vo.; Cloth,* $1.25; *Paper,* 75c.

AT ALL BOOKSELLERS, OR SENT POST-PAID
BY THE PUBLISHERS

The Black Douglas. By S. R. CROCKETT.

This is a romantic and stirring story of the fifteenth century with its armed strongholds and its fighting men. Lovely women are also to be found in the tale, and their influence on its development is strong. *Crown 8vo., Cloth, $1.25 ; Paper, 75 cents.*

Agriculture. By C. C. JAMES, M.A., Dep. Min. of Agriculture for Ontario.

Authorized for use in schools. As a primary treatise in the science underlying farming, no better treatise has been put before the public. *Crown 8vo. Cloth, 25 cents.*

Away from Newspaperdom and other Poems. By BERNARD McEVOY.

The style and the sentiment of the poems are admirable. Mr. McEvoy has both the eye and ear of the true poet. *Square 8vo., with illustrations by G. A. Reid, R.C.A. Cloth, $1.00 ; Paper, 50 cents.*

Canada and Its Capital. By SIR JAMES EDGAR, Speaker of the Dominion House of Commons.

Containing twenty-one photogravure illustrations. "The work is a beautiful production from all points of view. Contains material that is calculated to make Ottawa the Mecca of the tourist, the sportsman, and the health-seeker." *Large 8vo., Cloth, $2.50 ; half-Morocco, $3.50.*

A History of Canada. By CHARLES G. D. ROBERTS, Author of "The Forge in the Forest," "A Sister to Evangeline," etc.

A complete history, with chronological chart and maps of the Dominion of Canada and Newfoundland ; containing nearly 500 pages, including appendix, giving the British North America and Imperial Acts in full. *Large 8vo., Cloth, ornamental, $2.00.*

The Book of Games : with directions how to play them. By MARY WHITE.

As a compendium of evening amusements for the family and other social circles it is unrivalled. *Cloth, ornamental, 12mo., $1.00.*

AT ALL BOOKSELLERS, OR SENT POST-PAID BY THE PUBLISHERS

Where Dwells Our Lady of the Sunshine. By the COUNTESS OF ABERDEEN.

A booklet describing the grand resources of Canada, in the form of a parable. *Square, 16mo., deckle edge cover, with design in gold. 10c.*

The Incidental Bishop. By GRANT ALLEN.

This is a bit of good literary sculpture, the scene of which is laid partly in Africa and partly in Britain. *Crown 8vo. Paper, 50c.*

Bachelor Ballads. By BLANCHE McMANUS.

This is an attractive book, containing 29 of the celebrated good fellowship songs of the world. *Crown, 8vo., bound in art linen, with numerous illustrations, $1.50.*

Equality. By EDWARD BELLAMY, a sequel to "Looking Backward."

The large sale which this book has had indicates that its subject is an interesting one. *Crown, 8vo.; Cloth, $1.25; Paper, 75c.*

The Scourge of God. A Novel, By JOHN BLOUNDELL-BURTON, Author of "The Clash of Arms," "The Mutable Many," etc.

This is an engrossing story of religious persecution. *Crown, 8vo.; Cloth, $1.00; Paper, 50c.*

When the World was Younger. By MISS M. E. BRADDON.

An historical romance of the Stuart period, in which love, tragedy, and passion figure prominently. *Crown. 8vo.; Cloth, $1.25; Paper, 50c.*

The Deluge. By HENRYK SIENKIEWICZ, Author of "Quo Vadis," etc.

This work completes the trilogy begun by the author's great novel, "With Fire and Sword," of which "Pan Michael" also forms a number. It deals in a masterly way, with Russian and Polish history. *2 vols. Crown 8vo. Cloth, $1.25; Paper, 75c.*

*AT ALL BOOKSELLERS, OR SENT POST-PAID
BY THE PUBLISHERS*

Wild Animals I Have Known. By ERNEST SETON THOMPSON, Naturalist to the Government of Manitoba, Author of "Birds of Manitoba," etc.

This book has fair claims to being considered unique, for it is probably the first serious attempt to depict the daily life of wild animals as it really is. *Profusely illustrated by the author. Cloth, octavo, $2.00.*

Miss Grace of All Souls. A novel, by WILLIAM EDWARDS TIREBUCK, Author of "St. Margarets," "Sweetheart Gwen," etc.

Its scene is laid in one of the mining districts of England, and social conditions are touched upon in a discerning and sympathetic manner. *Crown 8vo. Cloth, $1.00 ; Paper, 50c.*

The Wonderful Century. By ALFRED RUSSEL WALLACE, Author of "The Malay Archipelago," "Darwinism," etc.

This book describes the doings of science during the century that is now drawing to a close, and also touches upon their relation to social conditions. It is a most interesting review of electricity, travel, labor saving machinery, evolution, etc. *Crown 8vo. Cloth, $2.00.*

Her Memory. By MAARTEN MAARTENS, Author of "God's Fool," "Joost Aveling," etc.

The delicate and finely sympathetic quality of this consummate literary artist is well illustrated in the revelations and finished characterizations of this novel. *Crown 8vo., with portrait of the author: Cloth, $1.50 ; Paper, 75c.*

In the Forest of Arden. By HAMILTON W. MABIE, Author of "Essays on Work and Culture," "My Study Fire," etc.

This is a beautiful piece of poetic idealism, and is presented to the public in a dress in all respects worthy of its literary beauty. *Large Crown 8vo., Cloth and Gold, Gilt-top, decorated by Will H. Low, Edition de Luxe, $2.25.*

AT ALL BOOKSELLERS, OR SENT POST-PAID BY THE PUBLISHERS

Notes on Appreciation of Art and on Art in Ontario:
With remarks on the Exhibition of the Ontario
Society of Artists, MDCCCXCVIII. By JAMES
MAVOR.

*12mo.; Paper, with eleven illustrations from original draw-
ings by the artists, 25c.*

At the Cross Roads. By F. F. MONTRÉSOR, Author
of "Into the Highways and Hedges," "False
Coin or True," etc.

There is as much strength in this book as in a dozen ordinary
successful novels. *Crown 8vo. Cloth, $1.00; Paper, 50c.*

The United States of Europe, on the Eve of the
Parliament of Peace. By W. T. STEAD.

This is a most interesting description of a tour around
Europe by the Author, in the fall of 1898. It is lavishly and
beautifully illustrated. *Crown 8vo., Cloth, $1.50.*

The Confounding of Camelia. A Novel, by ANNE
DOUGLAS SEDGWICK.

This is a story of English life and society, which attracts by
its truth and intimateness. *Crown 8vo., Cloth, $1.00; Paper, 50c.*

Love Among the Lions. By F. ANSTEY, Author of
"Vice Versa."

A very bright little story of a strange matrimonial experience, with thirteen clever illustrations. *12mo.; Paper, 50c.*

Scottish Folk Lore, or Reminiscences of Aberdeen-
shire, from Pinafore to Gown. By REV. DUNCAN
ANDERSON, M.A., Author of "The Lays of
Canada," etc. *12mo.; Cloth, $1.00.*

---

*AT ALL BOOKSELLERS, OR SENT POST-PAID
BY THE PUBLISHERS*

GEORGE N. MORANG & COMPANY'S LIST.

The Celebrity. By WINSTON CHURCHILL.

This is an exceedingly amusing book. All the characters are drawn with the firm sharpness of a master hand. To read "The Celebrity" is to laugh. The dramatic effects are unforced. *Crown, 8vo.; Cloth, $1.00; Paper, 50c.*

Commercial Cuba: A Book for Business Men. With eight maps, seven plans of cities, and forty full page illustrations. By WILLIAM J. CLARK, of the General Electric Company, with an introduction by E. SHERMAN GOULD, M. Am. Soc. C. E.

Octavo; Cloth, $4.50.

Lyrics of Lowly Life. By PAUL LAWRENCE DUNBAR.

A very pleasing collection of short poems by a rising writer. *Cloth, 12mo., $1.25.*

Folks from Dixie. By PAUL LAWRENCE DUNBAR, illustrated by E. W. KEMBLE.

In the present work the author comes before us as a successful writer of short stories and graphic sketches of negro life. These pages are replete with humor. *Cloth, 12mo., ornamental, $1.25.*

The Science of Political Economy. By HENRY GEORGE, Author of "Progress and Poverty," "Social Problems," Etc.

This is the last work of the celebrated author. In his introduction he calls it "a treatise on matters which absorb the larger part of the thought and effort of the vast majority of us—the getting of a living." *Crown, 8vo., Cloth, $2.00.*

Little Masterpieces. From HAWTHORNE, POE and IRVING.

These volumes comprise the most characteristic writings of each author, carefully selected and edited by Prof. Bliss Perry, of Princeton University. *Flexible cloth, 16mo., gilt top, 3 vols. in a box. per vol. 40c.*

AT ALL BOOKSELLERS, OR SENT POST-PAID BY THE PUBLISHERS

The Choir Invisible. By JAMES LANE ALLEN.

The longest, strongest and most beautiful of Mr. Allen's novels. *Crown 8vo. Cloth, $1.25; Paper, 75c.*

A Kentucky Cardinal and Aftermath. By JAMES LANE ALLEN.

"A Kentucky Cardinal" and "Aftermath," form, together, one of the most delightful little love stories that was ever written. *12mo. Cloth, $1.25; Paper, 75c.*

Simon Dale. By ANTHONY HOPE ; with eight full-page illustrations.

The story has to do with the English and French Courts in the time of Charles II. The material for a tale of love, intrigue and adventure to be found here, could hardly be surpassed. *Crown 8vo. Cloth, $1.50; Paper, 75c.*

Rupert of Hentzau. By ANTHONY HOPE, a Sequel to "The Prisoner of Zenda," illustrated by CHARLES DANA GIBSON.

The world is always ready to read a story of courage and daring, and there is even more exemplification of these qualities in "Rupert of Hentzau" than there was in "The Prisoner of Zenda." *Crown 8vo. Cloth, $1.50; Paper, 75c.*

Paris. By EMILE ZOLA.

The descriptive power of the author is so great that to read this is to take a bird's eye view of the things and people described. The political world is unveiled for us and Parisian journalism is drawn with a keen pen. *Crown 8vo. Cloth, $1.25; Paper, 75c.*

The Christian. By HALL CAINE.

This book deserves a fresh interest from its recent dramatization under the superintendence of the author. No novel of recent years has aroused more discussion, and none has been read with greater eagerness. *Crown 8vo. Cloth, $1.50 ; Paper, 75c.*

The Beth Book. By SARAH GRAND, Author of "The Heavenly Twins."

Sarah Grand's new work of fiction "The Beth Book," will be likely to meet a wider acceptance than "The Heavenly Twins." As a literary production it fully sustains the anthor's high reputation. *Crown 8vo. Cloth, $1.50; Paper, 75c.*

AT ALL BOOKSELLERS, OR SENT POST-PAID
BY THE PUBLISHERS

Caleb West. By F. HOPKINSON SMITH.

This remarkable story is full of human nature and incident. It has had a surprising run in the United States, and describes the exigencies that an engineer had to meet with while building a lighthouse on a stormy coast. *Crown 8vo. Cloth, $1.50; Paper, 75c.*

The Grenadier. A Story of the Empire, by JAMES EUGENE FARMER.

Although this story is by a new writer, its force and ability mark it as the work of a coming man. It is a fine specimen of military fiction. *Crown 8vo. Cloth, $1.50 ; Paper, 75c.*

The Uncalled. A New Story, by PAUL LAWRENCE DUNBAR, Author of "Folks from Dixie."

This is a strong work of great interest, and will make its author a large number of friends. He writes what is in his heart, and has no mercy for sanctimonious shams. *Crown 8vo. Cloth, $1.25; Paper, 75c.*

The House of Hidden Treasure. By MAXWELL GRAY, Author of "The Silence of Dean Maitland," etc.

The success of the former works of this clever author guarantees a large sale of this novel. The portrayal of the character Grace Dorrien is a masterly effort, and there are scenes in the book that dwell in the memory. *Crown 8vo. Cloth, $1.50; Paper, 75c.*

Tekla. By ROBERT BARR.

This novel is pronounced by competent critics to be its author's strongest work. As he is a Canadian, the book is sure to arouse strong interest. *Crown 8vo. Cloth, $1.25; Paper, 75c.*

With The Black Prince. By W. O. STODDARD. Illustrated.

This is an ideal boy's book. It deals with a stirring period of history in a way that will captivate the boy's heart. *Crown 8vo. Cloth, ornamental, $1.50.*

AT ALL BOOKSELLERS, OR SENT POST-PAID BY THE PUBLISHERS

CPSIA information can be obtained
at www.ICGtesting.com
Printed in the USA
BVHW042316150223
658635BV00010B/173